AF395819

B-29 Superfortress

Dedicated to the late Professor J.E. "Jack" Spence OBE, Professor Emeritus and Head of War Studies at King's College, London, who gave his support during the writing of this book from its beginning to its completion.

The greatest of minds, and the greatest of friends.

B-29 Superfortress

Strategic Air War in the Pacific

Peter Saxton

Pen & Sword
AVIATION

First published in Great Britain in 2026 by
Pen & Sword Aviation
An imprint of Pen & Sword Books Limited
Yorkshire – Philadelphia

ISBN 978 1 03614 823 2

A CIP catalogue record for this book is
available from the British Library.

Typeset by Mac Style
Printed in the UK by CPI Group (UK) Ltd, Croydon, CR0 4YY.

The Publisher's authorised representative in the EU for product
safety is Authorised Rep Compliance Ltd., Ground Floor,
71 Lower Baggot Street, Dublin D02 P593, Ireland.
www.arccompliance.com

For a complete list of Pen & Sword titles please contact:

PEN & SWORD BOOKS LIMITED
47 Church Street, Barnsley, South Yorkshire, S70 2AS, England
E-mail: enquiries@pen-and-sword.co.uk
Website: www.pen-and-sword.co.uk
or
PEN AND SWORD BOOKS
1950 Lawrence Road, Havertown, PA 19083, USA
E-mail: uspen-and-sword@casematepublishers.com
Website: www.penandswordbooks.com

Contents

Chapter 1	Conduct of the Strategic Air War in Europe	1
Chapter 2	Geopolitics and Strategies	15
Chapter 3	Enter the Carriers	19
Chapter 4	The Coral Sea	27
Chapter 5	Midway	35
Chapter 6	The Philippines and Leyte Gulf	49
Chapter 7	Island Hopping	61
Chapter 8	The Boeing B-29 Superfortress	67
Chapter 9	Strategic Bombing	75
Chapter 10	A Surfeit of Options	87
Chapter 11	Making Choices	97
Chapter 12	Epilogue	101

Chapter 1

Conduct of the Strategic
Air War in Europe

The United States Army Air Force (USAAF) was formed from the US Army Air Corps in June 1941. This was intended to be a functional distancing from the US Army enabling its own command structure to avoid being simply tactical in purview and allow scope and freedom to devise and execute operations that could include strategic striking. Strategic operations take place beyond attritional battles between the armed forces of warring nations. They involve battles of interdiction intended to destroy the means of making war at all – the factories, the roads, railways, the communication systems and the populations whose manufacturing endeavors make all these systems work to the benefit of those who control them.

The Luftwaffe was essentially a tactical organization. The need for a strategic capability had been envisaged; much technological skill and effort had been expended and might well have been successful. These included the Messerschmitt Me 264, the Junkers Ju 390 and the Heinkel He 177, two of them four-engine types. However, distances between the countries in Europe, from Britain to the hinterlands of Soviet Russia, were small compared to the vastness of the Pacific Ocean. As Hitler's overall plan was to conquer all those within Europe who were not declared neutral, tactical aircraft took precedence. Tactical aircraft such as the Junkers Ju 87

Sturzkampfflugzeug, abbreviated to *Stuka*, were relatively cheap. They fell comfortably within current technology and could be produced in large numbers. Long range aircraft were yet to reach a stage in development whereby they could combine strategic range with an effective war load. The German manufacturers tried to do this by developing more powerful engines for twin-engine machines, but this proved problematic, especially in terms of engine fires. A reliable aero-engine with adequate power output was not yet available to them, and this implied the current need for four-engine aircraft.

The British, having become increasingly frustrated by the shortcomings of their twin-engine bombers such as the Bristol Blenheim and the Vickers Wellington, had gone through the same trials, come to the same conclusions and, critically, had switched priority to the urgent development of four-engine, long-range strategic bombers such as the Handley Page Halifax and the Avro Lancaster.

A similar evolution was happening in the United States, which also abandoned trying to solve the range/payload equation with twin-engine aircraft. They too settled on the four-engine formula, which, after the trials and tribulations of development, resulted in the Boeing B-17 Flying Fortress and the Consolidated B-24 Liberator. The Germans, ever spreading themselves thinly on many fronts, settled for the time being for twin-engine, medium bombers alone, effectively ruling themselves out of long-range strategic options for the foreseeable future. They had to fight close to the enemy heartland to be effective. That was sufficient until they attacked the British. Then they came under the guns of state-of-the-art RAF fighters, which used their manoeuvrability to cut down the heavily- laden bombers and sometimes even had enough time to land, re-arm, re-fuel and attack the same bomber formations on the way back to their bases.

Tactical fighters do not need impressive range and endurance if they are fighting over their own territory, whether it be their own heartland or over that of a conquered country. In the case of Britain, the German escort fighters were not fighting over their own territory and would arrive at the battle zones sometimes with only 15 minutes of fuel in their tanks before they had to break off and return to base. This left their bombers unescorted and vulnerable to large numbers of radar-guided Hurricanes. Having failed to destroy the RAF they switched away from tactical targeting of airfields and destroying the enemy in the air, to strategic attacks. This was a blunder – the Luftwaffe should have continued to fight at the tactical level as RAF Fighter Command was close to the end of its tether. Now, it was given breathing space and within weeks was making good use of it. Luftwaffe bomber losses deployed on daylight raids became unsustainable, so they switched to night raids. It was a portent of similar things to come.

The bombing of Britain continued, but this time not directed at grinding down the RAF but bombing British cities, industrial sites, docks, population centres – targets more typical of strategic raiding, but vastly more diverse and able to absorb punishment. They did so with medium bombers accepting all the payload limitations entailed. They were forced to mount these raids in the hours of darkness to cut the losses of bombers and crews to within sustainable limits. The Luftwaffe was shackled by distraction at the highest level. Hitler, ever mentally dominated by *Ostpolitic,* and despite a non-aggression pact, was grimly committed to the conquest of Russia. The Luftwaffe's prowess was now delimited by budgets calculated to leave sufficient resources available for other campaigns given higher priority, not by industrial output itself. Inevitably, Hitler eventually cancelled his planned invasion of Britain – Russia was a higher priority for him.

The German ground and air forces had met with initial tactical success so impressive that it hid their strategic weaknesses. The Luftwaffe supported their own front line on the ground by breaking holes in enemy deployments, which could then be widened by massed armoured assault; and by defending their following ground units from enemy air attack. The warplanes could return to the relative safety of bases that were behind their front line and move forward with it as it advanced. So, while Germany did make progress with four-engine, long-range strategic bombers, there was no pressing conviction driven by a dire need. Such projects were referred to by eponymous nicknames like 'Amerikabomber', which given the far reaches of the North Atlantic Ocean must have seemed, literally, a long way off. Their efforts did meet with minor success in the form of long-range raids against Russian targets in 1944. They were not pursued. Ironically, the campaign to conquer Soviet Russia was one place where strategic attacks deep behind Russian lines made sense and could have made a difference to the outcome of that ultimately disastrous campaign. Finally, and much too late, there was a short-lived strategic campaign against Britain in early 1944. Named the 'Steinbock' raids, they were mounted as revenge raids at a high cost in men and machines. They were called off but not before they had significantly reduced the Luftwaffe's options when their attentions had to shift to urgent preparations for repulsing the Allies' invasion of the European continent. In the early part of the Second World War therefore, the lack of effective strategic bombing capability was common to all the warring nations. The decision by the Allies to remedy this capability and to give it priority; and the decision by the Axis powers by default not to do so, was one of the most important differences in strategy that ultimately decided the outcome of the most massive European war ever experienced.

As the air battles progressed, the British found themselves forced to address the same exigencies as their enemy had at the end of the Battle of Britain. RAF Bomber Command, ordered onto the offensive, also suffered grievous losses, forcing them to abandon day attacks and embrace the night. The RAF's strategic striking force had the ability to hone these skills with experience. They also had the support of ranks of scientists and technicians whose purpose was to improve their bombing accuracy at night and in the bad weather conditions that prevailed over Europe, especially in winters. They had at their back a large and diverse aircraft industry, able to turn its engineering genius to meet the exigencies of seemingly any situation and which produced a series of modern, potent warplanes. One of the very best of these was the Lancaster produced by the A.V. Roe company (Avro). These aircraft could carry prodigious war loads over very long ranges and Berlin was well within its radius of action. The strategic night attacks on German industrial centres, on transport and communication infrastructure commenced and gathered momentum.

In the wake of the Japanese attack on Pearl Harbour on Hawaii, American airmen started to arrive in Britain. President Franklin Roosevelt had discussed with Prime Minister Winston Churchill the possibility of a general war between the democratic powers and the newly risen autocratic states of Germany, Japan, and Italy. They assumed that Spain, exhausted by civil war, would remain neutral but remain sympathetic to Germany, who had lent the winning side its air force in the Spanish Civil War. The newly formed Luftwaffe had played a pivotal role in the outcome of this war and gained for itself and Germany invaluable experience in the use of air power. Before the commencement of general hostilities therefore, Germany possessed a battle-hardened air arm which had evolved tactics they knew worked effectively. This brought with it a high level of confidence that they could prevail in the air and play their part in the combined ground-air offensives for which they had now become feared throughout Europe.

The USAAF took a completely different view from both the British and the Germans. They were commanded by a hard core of officers who were convinced that the future of air warfare, due to technological advances, was now at the point of evolving into a game changer with a capability that had not existed previously. The idea of strategic attacks was new neither intellectually nor practically. Zeppelins and heavy bombers such as the Gotha had carried out raids on the east coast of England in the First War, but the limits of technology at the time severely restricted what they could achieve. That was always going to change, and when it did the principles of war as expounded by officers and strategists such as Douhet in his work 'The Command of the Air' would be realised. This was the antithesis of the tactical doctrines embraced by the German armed forces in their driving conquests within continental Europe. It was also arguably at odds with thinking within the newly forming Allied armed forces, championed by sharp modernists such as Eisenhower, Tedder and Montgomery. These commanders were insisting on high levels of coordination between ground forces covered by airpower to support advance by protecting them from enemy air attack and by delivering ordinance to breach enemy strong points and formations. This thinking showed things in common with the Blitzkrieg model. Generals Ira Eaker, 'Hap' Arnold, Jimmy Doolittle and Curtis LeMay however, remained adherents of Douhet's theories that strategic bombing, of itself, could defeat an enemy by destroying its industrial, logistical and infrastructural might and thereby the means to prosecute war at all. In the event, both contending doctrines had merit and both doctrines were given a chance to prove themselves.

The strategic bombing strategy proved problematic. Firstly, the Americans found the development of a suitable aircraft was no easy task. There was the problem of limited engine power output, and even though American technology in supercharging was well to the fore it was still not enough. Thus, time and money was consumed experimenting to settle the twin or four engine question. Even when that was decided it was still not possible to get the war load to radius-of-action ratio near to what was needed.

The B-17 'Flying Fortress' was picked as the most suitable contender. It was a poor choice, based on assumptions about what an air campaign over Europe would be like. The B-17 had originally been designed as a coastal patrol aircraft, a tactically defensive role: strategic offensive missions were not part of its remit. At the test flying stage it did not perform impressively. The B-24 Consolidated Liberator, designed and built later than the B-17, performed rather better, but did not eradicate these problems, notably the critical bombload-to-range ratio. Both aircraft had similar space capacity in their bomb holds, which could accommodate around 8,000lbs weight in internally carried weaponry, but this was rarely used as it compromised the aircraft's range. The maximum bombload in a B-17 was reduced to just 5,000lbs to carry enough fuel to strike targets deep inside Germany and get back to England. Often it was less. This meant theoretically that nearly twice as many embattled sorties had to be flown to deliver any given level of destruction, which implied twice as many losses of crew and aircraft. The British Avro Lancaster, by contrast, typically carried a full 14,000lbs each mission and eventually could reach any target in Germany under protection of the night.

There were a number of reasons for such a stark difference in war load/range capability, and an important one was that the American massed day formation tactic required a lot of guns and a lot of armour, both very heavy items. The Lancaster was armed with rather fewer protective guns and almost no armour at all. To reduce this vulnerability therefore, the RAF chose night raiding. New in theatre and with no battle experience initially, the Americans started their raiding with tactics that were carefully thought out but so far untried.

The USAAF Command ignored the RAF's continuous advice to attack at night – it remained doggedly committed to daylight raiding. This decision included considerations about the new Norden bombsight that could give impressive results when dropped from a bomber that had acquired the target at least six miles away in perfect and cloudless visibility. The bomber had to be able to fly in a straight line for that time without being put off by flak or fighters. There was no attempt to develop blind flying suitable for European climate, where the ability to see the ground was the exception rather than the rule. The crews had to fly tight formations, almost wing tip to wing tip, initially each plane responsible for not colliding with any of the others that flew in such proximity. Minor heading corrections, necessary for collision avoidance, would degrade the Norden's accuracy. These aircraft had been developed, tested and 'proved' in meteorological conditions, for instance over the deserts of America, that were as different from European climate as is possible to imagine.

What was the plan to deal with attacking Luftwaffe fighters? The theory was that the massed formation of say 100 aircraft (though often far larger), 25 or more aircraft across and layered four deep, would be able to deal with fighter opposition. After all, each aircraft was toting thirteen heavy calibre machine guns placed dorsally, ventrally, rearward and laterally. Laterally, the gunners fired out of open hatches on either side of the fuselage. They had to endure seriously sub-zero temperatures for long periods of time. The pain of incipient frostbite and the misery of altitude sickness notwithstanding, they tried to bring a sight to bear on a tiny target that was coming at them at an unbelievable closing speed. It was usually in a 90-degree hard-banked raking turn, with wing leading edges sparkling with tiny yellow muzzle flashes. Ventrally there was a 'ball-turret' – a tiny revolving plexiglass ball in which crouched a man who had to be small of size (not more than 5ft 3in) and who lowered himself into a large goldfish bowl slung underneath the roaring bomber to grasp the machine-gun handles with his knees up to his chest. There can be few more painfully uncomfortable, not to say undignified ways to go into battle than that. Once in, he couldn't get out unaided. Bailing out of a stricken bomber? Chances were poor.

Carnage ensued. The Allied fighter cover was ineffective because there was no single-engine Allied fighter with the radius of action of a bomber – or even close to it. So, a perfunctory show was enacted daily where the bomber formations would receive air cover only to the limit of the fighters' radius of action, just where they didn't need it. There would be no Luftwaffe opposition on that leg. The escort, at the limit of their radius of action, would then turn for home leaving the bombers to their fate. The Luftwaffe radar and operations directors knew where that would happen and had their fighter squadrons ready at cockpit standby, rearmed, refuelled, engines run up to operating temperature and shut down. They would then be 'scrambled' (battle take-off) and vectored to an up-sun attack position, and the slaughter began. This would happen typically twice on each raid – once on the way out and once on the way back. Two deadly battles had to be fought to deliver one strike and get home. Feinting tactics were employed to try to conceal the real target of the day, but the Luftwaffe were well deployed and rarely fooled for long.

The day-time strategic air war in Europe in the early 1940s was agonising and drawn out. It was fought by aircrew who showed more grit and self-sacrifice than even they would have thought possible of themselves. Cometh the hour cometh the men. Their aircraft were at best sub-optimal to address the task they were allotted. As stated, the bombers, critically, had to reduce war load to achieve the radius of action to deliver it. The increased number of sorties implied proportionately increased losses in men and machines.

The psychological damage to those involved is not widely recorded, but it is safe to assume it was extreme. In those days such things were simply not considered, let alone talked about. One exception that did attempt to portray this was the famous film *Twelve O'Clock High*. Produced by Darryl F. Zanuck, the film starred the actor Gregory Peck and described how his character, the tough and aptly named General Savage, was put in command of an under-performing bomb group and ordered to get its performance up to scratch. The previous commander had been deemed too lenient and sympathetic to the crews facing the arduousness of the job they had to do. The message from Savage was that it had to be done and the crews were better placed to fear him more than enemy flak and fighters. The crews responded to his harsh discipline and their achievements rose; but Savage suffered a catatonic collapse because of the stress to himself. The film, although still accessible today, is preserved in the US National Film Registry as culturally and historically significant. When the author of this book was a cadet officer in the Royal Air Force, *Twelve O'clock High* was still being used as a training film about excellent leadership.

This bloody cycle could not have gone on for ever at the pace it did. For the period that it did ensue however, as fast as bombers were shot down, US manufacturing prowess and the flight training schools kept pace. It was a deadly stalemate; but then came an intervention that turned the tide of the strategic air war over Europe in favour of the Allies. It came in the form of a single engine fighter with the range of a bomber.

The North Aviation P-51 ('P' designating a pursuit fighter) was a triumph of subtle technological development. This incorporated some ingenious design principles to reduce drag by delaying the point of breakaway encountered as air flows over an aerofoil – called 'laminar flow'. It also incorporated multi-purpose apparatus weight reduction. Using either centreline or wing-mounted jettisonable reinforced paper drop tanks enabled a prodigious volume of fuel to be carried by this small aircraft far beyond original requirements. These design aspects, taken together, raised the all-important range of these fighters to 1,800 miles – completely in a class of its own.

The P-51 had originally been optimised for low to medium altitude for tactical air-fighting and attacking ground targets. It excelled in the role. To make the difference as a strategic escort fighter however, this fighter had to be capable of prevailing in battles that required speeds and altitudes well outside its original design specifications. The problem was solved, almost as a casual afterthought, by a few test pilots with a roving brief to see if a mix-and-match approach could deliver advantage. The casual comment was that the P-51 airframe dynamics were outstanding, but the plane was dogged by the wrong power-plant. The recommendation was to remove the original engine, optimised for low to medium level combat, and replace it with a highly supercharged tested and proven unit. That unit was the Rolls-Royce Merlin, famously employed in the Hurricane, the Spitfire, the Mosquito and the Lancaster bomber. Casual or no, it was realised in time to make the difference in the strategic air war in Europe. In the transformed P-51 Merlin Mustang the Allies had a top-class dogfighter, capable of taking on the best the Luftwaffe could send at them. It had a high top speed and rate of climb, a stall speed somewhat higher than considered normal but nevertheless forgiving, stability in a dive, and an operational ceiling above 30,000ft. It had the all-important range to keep with and above the bombers all the way out to the target, over the target, and all the way back to base in England. The P-51 Merlin Mustang was the only true strategic single-engine fighter of the entire war. It made the difference in sharply cutting the USAAF bomber aircraft and crew losses. It made the difference in the battle losses to the Luftwaffe which now had to contend with a dwindling number of deployable defensive machines and a critical reduction in experienced pilots to fly them.

This latter was a key intention within the overall strategic management of the war in Europe – to break the Luftwaffe in the air prior to Operation Overlord, the Allied invasion and liberation of Europe. A crucial tactical adjustment was ordered as these new long-range wonder planes started to fill the skies over Germany. General Jimmy Doolittle gave the message hard and clear to his fighter pilots – forget about protecting the bombers! That tactic put the Mustang pilots in a defensive frame of mind, which Doolittle was not going to tolerate. It also put them, potentially, at a height disadvantage relative to the enemy's attacking fighters. Don't stay with the bombers – get high above them and come down hard and fast into the Luftwaffe formations as and when they turn up for work. Shoot down their fighters and looking after the bombers will come of that.

The Luftwaffe was now in an inexorable downward trajectory towards becoming a spent force. It would be so before the Allied invasion of the continent began. It was the breakthrough that turned fortune in the Allies favour and enabled victory in the strategic air war being fought in the skies over Europe. This critically reduced losses of Allied soldiers and sailors during Operation Overlord.

For the rest of the war in Europe the partnership between RAF with its expertise in night raiding and the key reduction losses within the USAAF's day raiding operation proved irresistible. Strategic bombing had been overwhelming provided a realistic view was taken about what comprised combat advantage.

The lessons learned in the European theatre had to be internalised and translated to serve in the context of the climaxing Pacific war. The problems of height, range and payload, which, in the European strategic bombing war had been got right just in time, would have to be tackled to a greater degree of effectiveness before being applied to a war that was to be fought over and around an ocean and its coastal regions which extended over half of the globe.

Chapter 2

Geopolitics and Strategies

During the late 1930s, tensions between the United States and Imperial Japan increased. Both states saw each other as a competitor despite being separated by the Pacific Ocean, which itself occupied half the entire globe. Both sought a dominant position and to maximise its power and influence on the world stage. The United States, a former colony itself, was energetic in its efforts to acquire new territorial possessions of its own. It, for the large part, employed trade and diplomacy. Japan was desperate to see itself as a world power, and believed this could be achieved only by conquering other nations and annexing them into its own empire. It was a pattern that had emanated from Europe in the most recent centuries, but the coming of steel and explosives, industrial productive might and technological innovation, had enabled a manifold increase in the ability of those who had developed these abilities to dominate those who had not done so. In the sardonic summary of Hilaire Belloc –

> 'May God have mercy on this lot,
> Whatever happens we have got
> The Maxim gun and they have not'.

The history of the expansion of the United States is complex. Its own territorial expansion since independence was affected either by purchase, as for instance in the cases of Louisiana from the French and Alaska from Russia, or by armed force, as in the cases of the acquisition of territories previously part of the vast Spanish empire, which had been established since the 15th century in both American continents. A complex run of events over many years in the mid 19th century culminated in the Mexican American War and concluded with Texas being included as a state, the largest addition of territory in the contiguous grouping. They brought within the control of the United States territories that would largely comprise the future states of Arizona, California, Colorado, Montana, Nevada, New Mexico, Oklahoma, Oregon, Utah, Washington and Wyoming.

The US had also acquired huge trading interests around the Pacific western littoral, including China and the Philippines, which they had at least partially colonised at the end of the 19th century. It had close ties with Hawaii. It now claimed to be isolationist, but in a post-First World War context that was largely a precaution against becoming involved in any further wars in Europe.

The Japanese concluded that in terms of *realpolitik,* the international policies of the two countries were not very different. It was not very self-critical logic regarding methods employed. However, it did confirm they were in competition with one other and tensions between them grew apace.

Japan was seen by the United States as a belligerent power, hard to conclude otherwise given its recent history of invasions of China, Manchuria and French Indochina. The US responded with economic sanctions designed to curtail these expansions as a potential threat. The critical difference was that USA territories were rich in untapped strategic resources, such as oil, iron and therefore steel, which Japan was not. This provided more reason why the Japanese were desperate to expand further. They needed to acquire resources currently under the control of European powers.

In virtually all engagements before the battle for Midway the Japanese armed forces had met with indomitable success. In quick succession, they had driven the Americans out of the Philippines, the Dutch out of their colonies in the East Indies, and the British out of Malaya and Burma, Hong Kong and Singapore. Their new empire also included Manchuria, the north and west of China, the Korean Peninsula, Formosa (Taiwan), Hainan, French Indochina (Vietnam, Laos, Cambodia), Burma (Myanmar), Siam (Thailand), Borneo, Java, Sumatra, the Celebes, and many smaller island territories.

Their expansion into the western Pacific had several major purposes. It would give them access to the mentioned unlimited war resources; to exploit their peoples economically; and to build a defensive ring around their homeland. It also gave them the ability to interdict the shipping routes, which were key lines of communication for Allied trade and the sinews of their empires. These remaining open routes were from the United States to Australia and New Zealand; from Australasia to Ceylon and India; and thereon west to Europe, the Middle East and Africa via the Suez Canal or the Cape of Good Hope. With Malaya and Burma captured, the Japanese as close as Rabaul and with footholds in West Timor and New Guinea, Australia itself was threatened.

The Japanese seized the Solomon Islands to the northwest of Australia in May 1942. This proved to be the limit of their expanding circumference. These conquests added roughly one million square miles of exploitable territory to the Axis powers, equaling the size of the area conquered by Germany, and making a total area of 3.5 million square miles. Axis dominated populations totaled 321 million. The Allies dwarfed these statistics with populations of 1,300 million and territories of 30 million square miles. The figures were in favour of the Allies, but it was now a question of organization and sacrifice.

Chapter 3

Enter the Carriers

The United States was building aircraft carriers. This had been noted by Japan, who benefited from the fact that it had been a difficult birth. The armed forces of the early part of the 20th century had their die-hard conservatives, convinced that their current naval formulations were optimum and there was no funding to waste on untested innovation such as submarines or aircraft. Best stick to what was tried and tested and not lose focus.

There was a grudging concession about aircraft, however. Even top Generals such as John J. Pershing, an artillery officer, had mentally acknowledged the value of aircraft spotting fall of shell and signaling adjustments back to the gunners. However, as important as this and other auxiliary functions may have been to the outcome of a battle, they remained auxiliary and could hardly claim any form of strategic importance. They were contradicted, literally, by a new school of army officers who, inspired and energized by these new machines, refused to believe that such an innovation should be denied the full opportunity of development and realization of potential. They became slow-smoldering firebrands and had volunteered for flying training themselves. They argued that, given time and development, aircraft could fledge as strategic weapon systems able to deliver critical interdiction to the supply lines of armies. They were not afraid to fight their corner even though this involved the dangerous public contradiction of supreme commanders.

The first important outbreak was led by US artillery officer General William 'Billy' Mitchell. Mitchell, however, did not choose to focus on the interdiction of army supply lines, but focused on a naval scenario – the most controversial it was possible to imagine at the time. This embraced the conviction that the Titans of all modern navies – the armoured battleships – might be fatally threatened by such delicate machines. But like the Titans of myth and legend, they were former gods, about to be displaced by beings mightier. Mitchell and his cohorts not only thought it, they believed it fervently and were willing to give voice to it no matter how senior the rank of the man in front of them. They also began talking to the American press.

The powers decided to put the end to all this uncertainty and wayward behaviour by allowing the proposition to be put to the test. This was not to be credited to an intention of fairness or a devotion to evidence-based decision making. It was based on supreme confidence that such tests would prove them right and these maverick aviators wrong. This did not stop the high command trying to rig the tests in their favour, just in case a fluke result might suggest they were wrong. They set arbitrary rules for the demonstrations that placed the simulated air attacks on a ship at a critical disadvantage.

Mitchell, who had been banned from taking part in the tests, saw these rules were an attempt to determine the outcome and quietly retaliated by taking counter measures in terms of weights of bombs carried and ordering deliberate proximity explosions. Only direct hits could be counted according to the rules, set in ignorance of the fact that near proximity explosions could do as much damage as direct hits – and always below the waterline.

The target ship selected was a surrendered First World War German battleship named the SMS *Ostfriesland*. On 21 July 1921, Mitchell's handpicked aviators, using only six 2,000lb bombs, sent the battleship to the bottom thereby dispelling the myth of the invulnerability of the battleship to airpower. Ironically, this was repeated at Pearl Harbour on a disastrous scale 20 years later. To press home the point, the Japanese attacking aircraft were launched from aircraft carriers. This was a time when it became decreasingly credible for the American army and navy high commands not to recognize aircraft carriers as the new capital ships, having wrested that honour from the battleships of the day.

However, the Japanese made the opposite mistake of assuming that carriers could do anything, ignoring the restrictions on aircraft ordinance compelled by the need to get a fully loaded, single-engine aircraft off a perilously short carrier deck. Their opening move in the Battle of Midway was to try to neutralize the defensive infrastructure on the island itself, using carrier-based aircraft rather than closing with very heavy surface units such as the monster battleships the Yamato and the Musashi to bombard from the sea. The result was ineffective, and the Imperial Japanese Navy (IJN) task force decided in the heat of the moment to arm for a second land strike. This prevented the preparation and launch of the fighters that would now be needed to protect their fleet against the American torpedo and dive bombers probably being launched in retaliation and vectored towards them. Caught between the devil and the deep blue sea they were forced into the wrong choice, leaving their four carriers in the task force wide open to the US Navy strike, which duly arrived and sank three of their carriers, turning the tide of the battle.

Mitchell was famously court-martialed, demoted and sidelined. The nature and import of this piece of strategic wrong-headedness on the part of those at the very top of the US military and who held considerable sway over their political so-called masters, was depicted in the 1955 Otto Preminger film production *The Court-Martial of Billy Mitchell* starring Gary Cooper. He resigned his commission and died at the age of 56, a turbulent prophet before his time.

The Japanese attack on Pearl Harbour in December 1941 was a long-range, carrier-borne, pre-emptive air strike. It was attempting to seek out and destroy United States aircraft carriers to pursue its objective of naval domination of the Pacific and its shoreline countries. This misfired because the US carriers were not there – they were somewhere else in the reaches of the Pacific. On discovering this, their attacking airmen, with only minutes to get over the shock that their primary targets were missing from Pearl Harbour, took their only alternative – to attack whatever warships were moored there. Reduction of the infrastructure of Pearl Harbour itself might have been a strategic alternative but could not have been easily done by carrier strike. It might have been achieved by sustained battleship salvoes. The Japanese Navy had the two heaviest naval units of the entire war in the breath-taking battleships Yamato and her sister ship Musashi. Weighing in at 65,000 tons – nearly twice that of the battleships of other naval powers and with eighteen inch main armament, they should have been successful. If so, it would have had a critical effect on US abilities to mount the forthcoming carrier battles at the Coral Sea, Midway Island, and Leyte Gulf. Fortunately for Pearl Harbour and the US Navy, it was not the option preferred by the Japanese High Command.

In tactical terms, the Pearl Harbour attack was well executed. The need for surprise meant that the Japanese navy had to arrange for a large carrier task group complete with destroyers, cruisers and battleships to depart from ports in Japan in a way that was not too noteworthy. These separate units needed to disappear over the horizon, rendezvous and form up, and remain undetected crossing half of the largest stretch of ocean in the world. This they did, and their timing, to be in cahoots with diplomatic dissembling by Tokyo, went without flaw. But, in operational terms, the plan *was* flawed because they also needed either direct target reconnaissance from submarines, or accurate intelligence reports from agents on the ground. Confirmation that the position of the United States carrier fleet was where they presumed it would be was essential. This they did not achieve, a failure that brought nemesis on a scale that had not been anticipated. It delivered a reason for President Franklin Roosevelt to bring a formerly isolationist United States into the Second World War.

War declared, the threat from Japan now existential, certain strategic exigencies demanded maximum effort. Unlike in Europe there would be no slugging it out with opposing bomber commands wrecking each other's key cities and industries from their respective homelands – the distances were too vast. As the first strategic battles would therefore be naval in the Pacific, the issue of aircraft carrier dominance came immediately to the fore. Carrier dominance to establish air supremacy in the skies in the proximity of any US operation, whether it be ships at sea or any land invasion, became urgent to protect them from enemy air intervention. Air supremacy also presented opportunity for supporting attacks of ground designated enemy targets to reduce enemy concentrations of force.

Carriers alone could not deliver an overall offensive strategy. Carrier-borne aircraft could not heft anything close to sufficient bombloads to deliver a decisive strategic blow to Japanese infrastructure and industry. The US mounted a raid anyway. The famous 'Doolittle Raid' on Tokyo, and other targets in Honshu, was launched from a lone carrier – the USS *Hornet* in April 1942. A squadron of specially lightened B-24 Mitchell medium bombers was chosen and would be led by Lt. Colonel Doolittle himself. These aircraft were stripped of equipment, guns, ammunition, navigation aids, anything not making a direct contribution to range or dropping a bomb on a target. Bomb sights were removed too – the bombing could be on opportunity targets and the bombload itself was reduced to 2,000lbs.

They were to be flown by a skeleton crew. Most importantly, every nook and cranny was fitted with auxiliary fuel tanks, which doubled the bombers' range to put them within strike distance of the main island of Honshu as soon as the carrier approached as far as it could without risk of detection. There could be no return to the carrier. Although the pilots had been hastily trained in landing on dummy decks (carrier sized decks painted on land tarmac runways), in this raid the carrier, to avoid detection, would be standing off too far for the attacking aircraft to return. The captain of each aircraft was ordered to make their own arrangements as to diversion airfields.

All sixteen aircraft launched on this raid did their job. They put US bombers in Japanese skies. All the aircraft, except one, crashed either into the sea out of fuel, or over land where many of the crews also perished. A few were taken prisoner. Some were publicly beheaded afterwards at the end of a terrible captivity. Of the aircrew who did not drown in the sea or die because of crash landing, few survived but some were given refuge and hidden by the local Chinese people. The occupying Japanese forces responded with monstrous retribution and some estimates claim that no less than 250,000 innocent civilians were put to death for assisting the airmen. The one surviving Mitchell made it to Russia where it landed safely. The Soviet Union had signed a non-aggression pact with Japan, which required them to confiscate the aircraft and imprison the crew. The Soviet Union allowed the crew mysteriously to 'escape' and, impossibly, to make it back to Allied lines.

The raid did no significant damage, but damage was not the point of the raid anyway. The attack was intended as a portent of things to come. Attacks on Japan itself would not come from carrier borne aircraft, but from land-based bombers. Japanese strategic planners had foreseen this possibility. The conquest of areas on mainland Asia where an enemy might launch heavyweight land-based bombers against Japan was an objective that helped to shape the formulation of the defensive aspects of their overall strategy. The Japanese military was usually good at learning the lessons demonstrated by other world-dominating nations. They had similar ambition, so why not copy and improve? Their army was schooled by the *Wehrmacht*. Their navy abided by the modus operandi of the Royal Navy, even to their uniforms. However, there was one lesson they did not learn well enough. As Winston Churchill remarked after the Battle of Britain concluded,

'The fighters are our salvation…'

The Doolittle Raid was token revenge in the immediate aftermath of Pearl Harbour and a boost to US morale. It was intended to shock the Japanese government and cow its people by doing what was thought impossible – attacking targets on the Japanese archipelago. This complacency had led to a denudation of fighter cover over Japan, a strategic mistake that would exact a terrible price. The US also tried attacking Japan from the west from mainland Asia, particularly China and Manchuria. This too proved ineffective in destructive terms. There had to be another way.

Chapter 4

The Coral Sea

In the context of the Pacific, there were no land-based heavy bombers available with ranges anywhere nearly long enough for the protagonists to attack each other's homeland from their own. Though less than ideal, initially one aerial strike option considered was to use carrier-borne aircraft. However, as the Doolittle Raid had emphasized, carrier attacks alone could not comprise an offensive strategy. Carrier operations could not launch enough aircraft with sufficient warloads to deliver war-winning, knock-out blows to war-making economic infrastructure.

The problem was the range-to-bombload ratio. Loads in bomber aircraft consisted of a combination of fuel and bombload. These commodities were both variable, but in combination inversely proportional within the aircraft's maximum take-off weight. If you increased range you needed more fuel, which implied less weight of bombs. If you wanted an increased bombload it was at the expense of fuel, which implied less range.

The Doolittle Raid itself was an extreme example of this, where the range requirement was so great that it reduced the bombload to the point of ineffectiveness. The best answer was a land-based bomber with sufficient power to lift a devastating bombload, fly to a target thousands of miles away, bomb it and return to its point of origin, or to an alternate land base with the capacity to turn it around for further attacks. The US tried attacking Japan from the west from mainland Asia, particularly China and Manchuria, but for the same reasons, the bombloads were insufficient to be effective.

The other option recommending itself in the prosecution of a war over a vast ocean speckled with tiny islands, was to capture the islands sufficiently close to Japan. The strategic objective, put simply, was to establish a logistically viable base close enough for a bomber to carry a sufficient load of both fuel and bombs. If it were possible to capture such islands and build airfields on them it could be a war-winning strategy.

But that would be easier said than done. These territories had been occupied and fortified by Japan during its expansion outward. This had been terrific by any standard. Following close on the heels of Pearl Harbour in December 1941, the American territories of Guam and Wake Island were overrun later that month, and the Philippine Islands attacked at the same time. The Philippines proved an order of magnitude more difficult to conquer due the sizeable number of US troops garrisoned there, and the Japanese army did not finish the campaign until May of the following year.

Meanwhile, by February, a Japanese invasion force had sailed fast and undetected towards the northeast extremity of Malaya and launched a seaborne invasion around the town of Kota Bharu. The British, the imperial masters of Malaya, had based their defence of the peninsular, including the invaluable island of Singapore at its southern tip, on two strategic assumptions.

Firstly, that a seaborne attack on Singapore from the south by heavy naval units was the only viable threat. It wasn't. The possibility of a land encroachment from north to south was deemed impossible because Malaya was a mountainous terrain covered by thick equatorial rain forest or, in the vernacular, jungle. This was deemed impenetrable. The north-south roads were rudimentary, crossed by rivers with light bridges liable to be washed away in the Monsoon season and on paper easily defended according to the British pillbox thinking. The roads could not carry heavy units such as tanks. The distances were prodigious and any advance down them would be at the speed of a fully-burdened walking soldier with all the accompanying difficulties that this implied.

The Japanese did some lateral thinking and decided that their soldiers would cycle instead – and mounted them on thousands of the ubiquitous bicycles available in Malaya, which moved the theoretical rate of unopposed advance from less than 10 miles a day to three times as much. The guns in Singapore, were like the guns of Aqaba in the First World War. In 1917, a force of irregular cavalry led by the then Captain T.E. Lawrence, a cartographer, strategist and intelligence officer, had neutralized these heavy guns by attacking them from a quarter on which they could not be brought to bear. Singapore's heavy guns pointed south out to sea and similarly could not be turned around to counter an attack launched down the Malay Peninsula. The Japanese army duly arrived, unmolested on the north bank of the Straits of Johor to await the surrender of a Singapore already reeling under the unopposed onslaught of Japanese air units.

The year 1942 also saw fierce jungle fighting in opposition to the Japanese invasion of Burma. The almost impossible problems posed by the terrain and by distance were overcome using special units, trained to cope with them. What is more remarkable, however, is that these were not small guerrilla units composed of what would now be called 'special forces', but battalion, even division-sized units such as General Orde Wingate's 'Chindits' under the overall command of the brilliant General 'Bill' Slim. They were the first army in history to be supplied and supported entirely by air drop.

The final major Japanese heave was in Java, then a colony of the Dutch, and, after liberation, renamed Indonesia. From this point onwards, while Japanese thrusts continued, the Allies had caught their breath sufficiently and as a result produced a gigantic increase in the rate of manufacturing technical, industrial and logistical war materiel. Within an admirably short time they could put credible forces into this vast theatre with a good chance of stopping what had previously seemed unstoppable. The Solomon Islands in 1942 and the Battle of Milne Bay in August of that year marked the first defeat of the Japanese army in the Pacific War.

But first came the sea battles to establish, manage and protect the logistic resupply lines and reinforcement of the troops who would have to fight their way ashore to displace the occupying Japanese armies. Without securing the surrounding seas, which included air supremacy over them, the Allies could not have taken back the occupied territories, and there would be no runways and no big bombloads. The island-hopping strategy would not have worked and the battles of Guadalcanal, Iwo Jima, Okinawa, would have been even more horrendous than they proved, and might well have resulted in defeat. The Philippines, where the Americans had lost an entire army commanded by General Douglas MacArthur, was a particularly sore point, and the harsh treatment of prisoners in the Bataan 'death march' focused the minds of the war planners.

This responsibility was global in extent. The supply lines, as described, extended from East Asia but had to be defended from attack all the way from the Pacific, across the Indian Ocean and through to Europe via the Cape of Good Hope or through the Suez Canal. They also extended eastward across the Pacific to the west coast of the United States and to the US east coast via the Panama Canal. Even with the Allied countries' industrial might working flat out it was a huge stretch. The decision-making must have been most difficult when there was not enough materiel to supply everywhere in two theatres of war adequately at the same time and tough prioritization decisions were necessary. Victory at sea remained a necessary condition to winning the entire Pacific war.

The US Navy began its counterattack in May 1942 with the Battle of the Coral Sea, a carrier battle which was a reverse for the Japanese. This was closely followed by the Battle of Midway in May, which was a decisive defeat in which the Japanese navy lost four of its carriers to America's one. Japan also lost a very high number of attack planes and fighters. Some commentators have stated that this was the turn of the tide in the Pacific, but that seems premature and was certainly not the view of the United States Navy. The 'Battle of the Factories' had not yet started to make itself felt. Meanwhile, the Japanese were forced to accept that, for the time being, plans for further expansion would have to be shelved until their fortunes took a turn for the better. They were now strategically on the defensive. To prevent the contraction of the newly acquired Japanese empire the IJN would have to hold back the US Navy at sea and ensure the resupply and protection of its many occupying garrisons of soldiers entrenched within hundreds of Pacific islands and territories.

The Battle of the Coral Sea was fought between 4 and 8 May 1942. This battle claimed firsts in naval history including the first time two carrier forces had engaged each other. It was also the first time two such forces of surface ships had fought over the horizon. The enemy vessels did not come within sight of each other. Consequently, the big guns remained silent. They fought using only their embarked aircraft at long range.

The Japanese armed forces were in the final phases of their expansion south-east to invade both the Solomon Islands and New Guinea and include those countries within its empire. They had the same consistent aims to exploit its people and its resources. The seizing of the resources and labour would pay for itself many times over to the huge benefit of the Japanese economy and wealth.

It was also to act as a springboard for a further invasion of northern Australia to prevent it from building runways for bombing operations against Japan's newly acquired southeastern territories. Although this was considered by the Japanese to be a strategically defensive operation to strengthen their southern perimeter, it did not seem so to the US and the Australians because it brought them within invading range of Darwin and the north coast of Australia. The IJN had assembled two fleet (attack aircraft) carriers, for striking purposes and an escort carrier to provide fighter cover to the ships of the task force and to the invasion itself. The task force was unaware that the increasingly effective US signals network, based in Hawaii, had cracked the Japanese codes with enough time to deploy their own carrier task force to intercept, along with an American and Australian cruiser force. This was an impressive use of intelligence.

In early May 1942, the Japanese had landed troops onto both New Guinea and the Solomon Islands. To their shock, they came under sudden and unexpected attack by aircraft from the carrier USS *Yorktown*. The IJN lost some vessels. The IJN, nonplussed, ordered its ships to abort the invasion and withdraw to the Coral Sea to regroup and concentrate on the new threat. The two fleets remained uncertain of each other's position for the next 24 hours. Despite the confusion however, the USN reconnaissance aircraft did manage to find, attack and sink the enemy's escort carrier. The battle group was now without fighter cover over it. Then, the Japanese also fixed the position of the enemy fleet and launched strike aircraft to give battle.

In the main clash, the Japanese fared better with damage to only one of its two fleet carriers – the *Shokaku*. The USN, however, sustained damage to the *Yorktown* but more importantly the carrier *Lexington* was badly mauled, set ablaze, and eventually scuttled. This was not a good result for the USN. However, it was also one of those strange outcomes where, as in the Battle of Jutland in the previous war, one side, the German High Seas fleet, gained a tactical victory based on numbers of ships sunk, but the strategic win went to the Royal Navy. Notwithstanding the numbers, the High Seas Fleet withdrew to home ports to be bottled up behind the Skagerrak by the Royal Navy Grand Fleet, never to put to sea again until after Germany surrendered. It had failed to break the Royal Navy's blockade and as US newspaperman Andrew King wrote –

"The German fleet has assaulted its jailer, but it is still in jail."

Although each side had lost a carrier, the IJN taskforce had lost its escort carrier and therefore the fighter air cover essential to complete what had now become an opposed invasion.

In consideration of this, the invasion was called off and the Japanese fleet withdrew. The loss of an escort carrier along with its aircraft, and the damage to the *Shokaku* also removed the possibility of them participating in the Battle of Midway which took place during the following month and could have proved critical to the outcome. Important morale considerations to both sides were that it was the first time the Japanese had been beaten at sea, proving that it could be done. They were not invincible. Coral Sea marked the limit of Imperial Japanese expansion – from now on their newly conquered empire would be contracting.

The IJN up to this point had been more than holding its own tactically but was frustrated that it was making little progress in its greater strategic objectives. The Pearl Harbour attack failed in its major objective of destroying the US carrier strength; nor did it completely wreck the harbour infrastructure. The US ship-building replacement rate ensured that the US remained little diminished as a major naval power. This had been confirmed by Coral Sea where its attempt to secure its own southeast perimeter while gaining more large areas of exploitable territory in the southwest Pacific was thwarted largely by the loss of a single escort carrier.

The dash for dominance had to be pressed home. If Japan could sink the three carriers that comprised the US carrier fleet in the next engagement, which secretly focussed on the Midway atoll, that in turn might become a new launch point for a further, and this time victorious, attack on Pearl Harbour. US naval air power in that region of the Pacific would be destroyed, and air supremacy would then pass back to the Japanese throughout the entire Pacific relevant to Japanese imperial objectives. Even if the US brought its Atlantic carrier fleet back to the Pacific, the scales would still be tipped decisively in Japan's favour and the US might even sue for peace.

Chapter 5

Midway

The US Navy signals code-crackers continued doing critical work. Reformed in 1942, a few weeks after the attack on Pearl Harbour, their mission was to ensure that the USN would never be caught out again. It was heavy going and ran continuously day and night, but their efforts were ingenious. The level of traffic indicated that an attack or campaign was being planned and seemed to be centred on somewhere or something referred to in code as 'AF'. They baited a trap. They suspected it could be a codeword for Midway.

Midway is a large tropical island situated at the extreme northwestern end of the Hawaiian archipelago, just east of the International Dateline. The whole group is about 1,500 miles long. US signals intelligence sent an order, in code, to Midway signals centre telling them to signal back in 'clear' (unencoded) that their freshwater production facility was out of action. This was done. It wasn't true. The Japanese duly intercepted them, who then passed the message on to their signals centre, in code, that 'AF' was having trouble producing fresh water. This was intercepted in Hawaii and decoded, confirming that 'AF' was indeed Midway. Further intercepts revealed the date selected, enabled the deduction of which units would be involved and even the direction from which the Japanese task force would approach.

For the Japanese this was a complex operation to put together because the IJN was planning a three-pronged thrust including a diversionary feint. Admiral Yamamoto, revered by his sailors and airmen, had designed the strategies that had bought success at Pearl Harbour, even though he had grave and, as it turned out, accurate misgivings about the wisdom of the attack. He was in awe of America's industrial potential and was fearful about the consequences. His skills had also been key in wresting the Philippine islands from the Americans.

The Admiral's self-confidence was tempered with an ability to be self-critical. Even with his four carriers and powerful surface fleet, Yamamoto knew he was still in the dark. He maintained the assumption that the US Navy had no clear idea of where any attack would take place and that they, the IJN, continued to hold the initiative while the USN occupied itself second-guessing possibilities. He also assumed, however, that three converging battle groups would be detected at some point and decided to try to fool the Americans by giving them a false answer to their problem. The most northerly thrust was, therefore, initially a feint. Intending this thrust to be detected, it would lure the American carriers to set heading for the Aleutian Islands off Alaska, which was US territory. If the USN fell for this, it would be at the critical cost of dividing its forces.

The second central thrust, meanwhile, would be the main body. It would close distance to attack Midway Island itself. Its purpose was to sink any surface shipping in the approaches to Midway, and to gain air superiority by engaging the American air forces in air-to-air combat, while launching its bombers to destroy the airfields on the island. Critically weakened, ran the logic, the US defending forces would be incapable of opposing the Japanese invading force embarked in troop ships and their escorting naval units. These would arrive as the third, southerly, thrust on the following day. Once the attack on Midway commenced the Americans would realize they had been hoodwinked and turn south at all speed to engage. The

Japanese northern force would then also turn south to pursue and to engage this US battle group.

Armed with the enemy battle plan passed to him by naval intelligence, Admiral Chester Nimitz, chief of the US Pacific fleet, deployed his battle group to wrong-foot them. On 4 June 1942, Midway came under attack and Midway signals reported the fact to Pearl Harbor. The Battle of Midway was underway.

How did the two fleets match up to each other on paper? The Japanese navy sailors and airmen had experienced battle, and, tactically, so far had always prevailed. They, and their officers, had full confidence in their Admiral. His airmen comprised a corps of tempered aircrew. Their battle successes were used to lead and teach. They were already teaching the techniques and tactical lessons learned to the upcoming new crews. They had the confidence of success against the USN gained at Pearl Harbour and Coral Sea. They had superlative equipment especially in defence of their carrier fleet in the form of the Mitsubishi A6M Zero fighter.

The key aircraft in a carrier fleet were not the fighters, which were tactical and defensive, but the strike aircraft, principally the dive bombers and the torpedo bombers. While strike aircraft needed to jink when presented with a ship that was firing back, they were at least spared the blindness of high 'g' turning, the neck-crunching pull-ups, the disorientation of inverted flight. Combat aerobatics were not their order of the day. Strike aircraft were what carrier operations were all about and they had to fly as fast as possible, carrying as much as possible in fuel and high explosive. Comparison of the performance figures for carrier-borne strike planes were similar on both sides.

Not so with fighter planes. The performance of carrier fighters was critical when compared to those of the opposed enemy. The enemy fighters were trying to protect their own mother ship by staying within a patrol vicinity, while others would be escorting their own strike planes, which were trying to sink the enemy carrier. When two carrier forces closed trying to sink each other, they were engaged symmetrically – tactically almost a mirror image of each other.

All fighting vehicles comprise a trade-off between protection (armour), mobility (including manoeuvrability and range), and firepower. These tend to work against each other, so designers must seek a desired optimum balance. If you make a heavily armoured, heavily gunned tank for instance, this will tend to be at the expense of its range, speed, and manoeuvrability.

The Zero fighter had been developed from a previous fighter type that had quickly become obsolescent as a rush of aircraft technology development engulfed the combatants. Of the two competing manufacturers that entered the competition to gain the manufacturing contract, Nakajima, withdrew. Its design engineers doubted that a machine with the required capabilities, within a reasonable balance of the standard objectives described above, could be produced given current technology. Technically, Nakajima was right. Mitsubishi decided that, as the project had been awarded to them by default, it was worth the risk and went to work.

The problem was how to produce an aircraft of competitive agility but at the same time to add sufficiently long range to the attacks. To do this from a carrier necessitated a restriction on its wingspan, which brought lift limitations. Mitsubishi did not achieve this combination by developing a new technology as North American Aviation had in the case of the P-51 Mustang with its invention of lamina-flow technology. It achieved it almost entirely by over-drastic weight reduction. Mitsubishi made a good start by using an innovative, secretly invented, very light aluminium compound for fuselage and wing structures. Mitsubishi also abandoned any attempt to carry pilot-protection armour and the damage limitation of self-sealing fuel tanks. As a result, the plane was in fact fragile – a single cannon round could disrupt it – not a good quality for a combat plane. It was a no-compromise solution which left little room for mistakes in a dogfight.

However, at dogfighting they were excellent, and, in the early part of the war, no Allied carrier fighter could match them. The Zero had a broad wing chord (width) to offset the loss of span and deliver a low wing loading bestowing other critical tactical advantages. It was blessed with a low stall speed of around 55 knots, which was an important safety point for carrier deck operations. Its ultra-light weight produced phenomenal manoeuvrability, easily beating any Allied fighters in a turning fight. The other purpose of the light weight was the ability to carry a lot of fuel, which meant an impressive radius of action (out and back). The Zero, with a radius of action of just under 1,000 miles, could range hundreds of miles away from the carrier, engage in an air battle or attack a surface target, then recover to the mother ship. No other fighter could do that to the same extent or even get close. If your scout planes reported there was a Japanese aircraft carrier within 800 miles of you, you needed to anticipate and prepare for an engagement.

Against this formidable lightweight the Americans deployed the Grumman F4F Wildcat heavyweight, the designation first 'F' standing for 'Fighter'. They had not created much choice for themselves, advances in technology having lagged behind events. It was a mid-wing radial, far heavier than the Zero, considerably slower, less agile and with a markedly shorter range capability. Tested in combat, it disappointed its pilots in both the battles of Coral Sea and Midway. Nevertheless, they made the best of it and chalked up shoot-down rates that theoretically should not have been expected.

The Zero's phenomenal manoeuvrability nullified the tactic of the turning fight to attack an opponent from the rear – a basic ploy up until then. It had to be abandoned as a losing manoeuvre. Allied fighters adopted the diving attack from above where speed advantage was theirs, opening fire as the range closed, and recovering in a full power, high-g pull-up to repeat the manoeuvre. This was not a new evolution, nor was it a complete answer as the Zero had a climb rate and angle of climb rate that were still the best, but it helped if you were above the enemy on first contact. Something more was needed for when you weren't.

An insightful squadron commander, Lieutenant Colonel Johnny Thach thought he had an alternative. He sketched it out and modelled the dynamics of it over bottles of beer with colleagues – on tabletops with matchsticks. They thought they had something new and exciting, so they went out, climbed into their Wildcats, and flew it. There didn't seem to be a flaw. Two aircraft would fly together in a loose line-abreast pair, covering each other. If an attack came from head on – the most dangerous position – the two Wildcats would turn towards each other. A single Zero had to concentrate on one of them, and as the tracks of the two Wildcats crossed it would become clear which of them that was. The second Wildcat would then be positioned to chop the Zero as he passed in front. Detractors were quick to point out that the Wildcats already had a numerical advantage. It did, however, reduce the possibility of a one-to-one turning fight, which the Zero pilot, given the agility of his machine, was probably going to win. Also, the principle that victory will go to the pilot who sees the other first still very much applied – and there were two pairs of Wildcat eyes to the Zero's one. The tactic was named 'The Thach Weave'. It was not a magic wand, but it narrowed the odds.

The Zero was a determined concept, stunningly successful at first, but the accelerating technical race for increased prowess in fighter performance outran Japanese development work due to the disruption of their industry and supply lines. This was when the B-29 strategic bombing finally began. The designating letter 'B' indicated that the aircraft was a bomber, and the B-29 was the most expensive and most technically advanced of the war.

In the meantime, the American fighter pilots' grumblings were taken seriously, and Grumman attempted to develop a derivative, which they named the F6F Hellcat. It was even heavier, bigger, had more armour, range, and increased firepower. Critically, this plane had an engine sufficiently powerful to outperform the Zero. It was not available until later in the war, when they operated from the big fleet carriers making way for the Wildcats to emplane in the smaller escort carriers.

At Midway, the USN deployed three fleet carriers – the *Yorktown*, the *Hornet* and the *Enterprise*. Unknown to the Japanese, Admiral Chester Nimitz based his battleplan on the almost certain knowledge that the main target for the Japanese was Midway, and not what the northern thrust was suggesting as the Aleutian Islands. The ruse had been negated by excellent intelligence. He assembled a battlefleet in the central Pacific, surprising everyone by appointing Admiral Raymond Spruance to command it. Spruance was a cruiser Admiral, not carrier, but when the most famous carrier officer – Admiral "Bull' Halsey – had been hospitalized with an acute, contagious skin condition he had been asked by Nimitz to name his replacement. Halsey chose Spruance, so Spruance had the kudos of being so blessed. The US fleet weighed anchor and steamed towards Midway, 1,000 miles west of Pearl Harbour.

The IJN was arming and preparing its aircraft for a strike on Midway. The exact position of the Japanese carrier fleet was unknown to the Americans. The air squadrons on Midway put up reconnaissance patrol aircraft principally the Consolidated PBY. The P and B stood for patrol bomber and the Y was designated to the manufacturer, The Consolidated Aircraft Corporation. When operated by the RAF, these planes were affectionally named 'Catalina' as a salute to their designers and builders in California.

The Catalina was an ingenious, twin-engine, amphibious patrol bomber, which reduced drag by designing the main sea-floats to retract outwards to form tip fences. Tip fences can be observed out of the window of airliners today as a matter of commonplace, but the retracting floats on the PBY were a pioneering early form. This helped give a jaw-dropping endurance of around 24 hours depending on conditions. Midway, a tiny spec in the vastness of the Pacific, was the last outpost for the Americans between Japan and Hawaii.

Catalinas continued to fly out in a fan of tracks hoping to locate the Japanese fleet that they knew was inbound. The first sighting was of the transport group to the south, but after careful consideration of its composition, it was concluded, correctly, back at Pearl Harbour that this could not be the main body of the attacking fleet. The search was concentrated further north. The Japanese main battle fleet included the four carriers that had attacked Pearl Harbour the previous December. Admiral Yamamoto had commanded them on that occasion too. There was a general air of confidence.

The Japanese bombers and dive-bombers, escorted by Zero fighters, were launched and headed towards Midway in formation. The attack was devastating yet not decisive, and it remains a puzzle why the fleet battleships were not used for such a bombardment, which probably would have been. The air forces based on Midway fought back hard, including B-17 Flying Fortresses bombing from altitude to minimize the lethality of the anti-aircraft fire coming up at them from the ships below. The Japanese carriers executed a series of well-practiced hard turns which successfully frustrated the aiming of the American bombardiers. After the planes broke off for home to refuel and rearm, not one Japanese carrier had been hit. Meanwhile the invasion group was closing in, anticipating a landing on Midway as soon as they approached the designated beaches.

The carrier groups of Japan and the US closed the distance between them sufficiently to launch air attacks and an intense carrier battle ensued. Planes from both sides attacked each other, recovered to their mother ships to rearm, refuel, and launch again to inflict further attacks. There were heavy losses on both sides, but the tally started to go against the IJN fleet from early on. Based on the reports from their squadron commanders that the reduction of Midway's ability to resist the invasion was incomplete, Admiral Yamamoto had ordered his carriers to rearm for further attacks to bomb Midway.

The timing was disastrous for the Japanese. The US carriers had located the Japanese main body and were at full speed to engage. The Japanese carriers were in the process of rearming their planes for the second attack on Midway. They had planes on their decks bomb-loaded for a land strike rather than with bombs optimized for a sea fight and torpedoes. They were caught flat-footed and would pay a big price. As American torpedo and dive bombers approached their targets there was a frantic rush on the Japanese carriers to get as many Zeros in the air as possible, while at the same time, rearming their strike planes. This entailed taking off the land-strike bombs and rearming them with torpedoes or bombs optimized for anti-shipping. The protective fighters, some of which had been on standing patrol since the first launch to attack Midway, also had to be recovered to ship, rearmed and refuelled, adding to an already dire and complicated situation where mistakes in process management would invariably go badly wrong. The discarded bombs could not be secured in safe stowage – there was no time – and these were left littering the decks and hangars.

USN Scout Bomber Douglas (SBD) Dauntless dive-bombers droned in. They began as specks in the sky becoming larger by the second. Some penetrated the fighters and attacked, concentrating on the Japanese carriers. The Japanese fighters that were still operational and with enough fuel for a fight stayed airborne and fought hard. Despite their depleted numbers, they shot down many of the US dive-bombers coming at them. One squadron of Grumman Avenger torpedo bombers was all but annihilated and only two fliers survived. It is said that Admiral Yamamoto himself was impressed by their bravery and saddened at their loss. No hits were achieved in this wave of the attack. Out of a total of forty- one torpedo bombers launched from the US carriers, only six survived to return to their ships.

The next phase was composed of waves of dive-bombers, arriving close behind. In contrast to the wave-hopping torpedo bombers, they approached at high level diving down on the carriers at an angle of 80 degrees. The pilots were literally steering the bombs at their targets down to the bomb release height, which in air bombing terms was point-blank range.

Ideally, they should have arrived at the same time as the torpedo bombers to attempt to overwhelm the target ship's defences drawing fire away from the lumbering torpedo planes. That had not happened. After bomb release, the pilot hauled the aircraft into a high 'g' pull out, flashing over the ship and probably banking in a hard turn to avoid presenting himself as a steady, no deflection, easy target. The anti-aircraft guns ran themselves red-hot and took their toll; the Japanese fighters, running out of fuel to the point of ditching, continued desperately to intervene and achieved some success, but it was not enough. Two of the carriers were mortally damaged.

The effect of the USN bombs was magnified catastrophically by explosions of the unsecured Japanese bombs, which had been hastily abandoned, on the decks and down below, in the rush to rearm with torpedoes. The carrier *Akagi* was the first to be put out of the fight as it started to sink, its listing decks making further air operations impossible. The carrier odds had now been made equal – three against three – but not for long. The carrier *Kaga* was crippled shortly afterwards, slowed, and it too started to sink.

The American carrier force now outnumbered the Japanese three to two. Underneath all the mayhem an American submarine, which had, with impressive seamanship, managed to keep in touch with the fast-moving task force, brought the carrier *Soryu* into the cross hairs of its periscope and fired torpedoes. They struck home and the *Soryu* too fell out of the fight, starting to sink. This left only one Japanese carrier operational – the *Hiryu*. This reversal of fortune had taken place little more than five minutes – an astonishingly short space of time, and testimony to the ferocity of the fight between these seven carrier behemoths.

The news, signalled back to Pearl Harbour, caused shouts of jubilation. Here was a great victory and it called for nothing more to claim it so. The smart advice now was to pull back the US carriers immediately rather than take any more risks. But Admiral Nimitz was having none of it. He was on a roll, and he wanted the job finished. He wanted the fourth Japanese carrier sunk. The battle raged on.

Undamaged and fully serviceable, the *Hiryu* knew the day was a disaster but, to the way of thinking of Japanese navy fliers, discretion was not the better part of valour. Even more determined, they launched scout planes, which were successful in locating the carrier USS *Yorktown*. They immediately launched strike aircraft to attack the carrier. The *Yorktown* detected the Japanese air squadrons heading straight at them when they were just over forty miles away. That meant less than fifteen minutes' flying time to the commencement of the incoming attack. The *Yorktown's* fighters were launched and they, with the carrier anti-aircraft gunners, fought grimly, but could not prevent the carrier coming under mortal attack. On fire, and trailing a huge smoke plume, she started to sink. She was a long time in the dying.

The other American carriers now turned to try to take the pressure off the *Yorktown*. Aircraft from the USS *Enterprise* raced towards the *Hiryu* to cut off the threat at its source. *Hiryu*, the only surviving Japanese carrier, responded with two waves of attacks—both times bombing the USS *Yorktown*, still afloat. On the afternoon of 4 June, *Hiryu* was located by the *Enterprise*, which sent dive-bombers to attack. They left the *Hiryu* burning and without the ability to launch aircraft before it too finally sank. *Yorktown* was badly damaged, and a Herculean effort was made to save her. She was mercifully evacuated. She was finally torpedoed and sunk by a Japanese submarine.

If there had been some debate about whether the battle of the Coral Sea could be a turning point in the sea war, there could be no doubt now that the battle of Midway was. It was a signal victory for the USN but a severe blow to the IJN, enfeebling their naval prowess by an irreplaceable loss of ships and valuable experienced aircrews. US servicemen now believed they could win against an enemy so recently considered invincible.

Admiral Nimitz had sought and found the Japanese main body, refusing to be duped by the IJN northern force feint. He was briefed by excellent intelligence processes, which had been reorganized and improved immeasurably since the Pearl Harbour attack. After the woe of Pearl Harbour, the US military organization and its intelligence network had shaken themselves to a position where a rolling series of sea victories was possible. After Midway, strategic exigencies increasingly made themselves felt. Japan's stretched economy and industrial capacities were unable to replace losses in equipment and trained men. The US's already massive industrial and training capabilities increased sharply and irresistibly.

Later that year, Admiral Yamamoto was killed in a transport plane shot down by US P-38 Lightning long-range fighters, once more under the guidance of USN Intelligence. Working only with intercepted flight plans, the intelligence gathered enabled the fighter pilots to intercept that single aircraft at a precise point at extreme range.

Chapter 6

The Philippines and Leyte Gulf

Beginning in August 1942, a series of carrier battles was fought that exceeded even the ferocity of Midway. As at Coral Sea and Midway, the belligerents were at long range over the horizon from one another. Part of the vast Melanesian archipelago, the Solomon Islands spread themselves across the trade routes between North America and Australia. As already described, Japan had invaded many islands such as these for the same reasons. They needed to exploit their natural resources and inhabitants; to neutralise any prospective base that might be used to attack their home islands in Japan; and, of immediate importance to the US, to interdict the US-Australian trade routes.

Three major islands within the group – Tulagi, Guadalcanal, and the Florida sub-group – were invaded by US Marines. It was the first major Allied invasion of the Pacific War and the beginning of the island-hopping strategy to relieve the sufferings of the conquered peoples and to cut the supply chains of the Japanese empire. If this could be achieved, it would disrupt the ability of the Japanese state to prosecute war at all. These were all strategic exigencies of which the prime one was to capture land to build and operate runways from which the new B-29 strategic bomber could strike at the Japanese islands themselves.

The grand plan had selected the Mariana Islands for this purpose. They were close enough but, before it could be effected, the Allies had to carry out the invasions of dozens of other Japanese occupied islands. This was needed to neutralise any future counterattack from the rear or by them interdicting the longest flank in history. The soldiers and marines of this first land thrust were supported, resupplied and protected by naval units and naval air units. Named the Guadalcanal Campaign, it was a joint service strategy requiring combined operations between land, sea, and air forces evolved painfully, but eventually successfully, in the European war.

The naval protection and delivery of the ground forces to their landing beaches was the responsibility of three task forces with a fleet carrier as the centre of each. Names emerged into the public consciousness that would ring with fame, such as *Enterprise*, veteran of Midway; such as *Wasp* and *Saratoga*. While the carriers with their emplaned air wings went about their business, they were ringed and protected by surface warships comprising six cruisers, two of which were Australian, many destroyers and a battleship. In overall command was Admiral Frank Fletcher, rested after Midway, who had chosen to hoist his flag in the USS *Saratoga*.

Prior to the fleet approaching the landing grounds the carriers launched a fighter 'cap' (Combat Air Patrol) providing air cover to both the naval and ground elements. The fleets of landing craft swept into their allotted beaches and the marines leaped into the surf. Ground attack aircraft flying in loose formations had already attacked ahead to soften resistance to the advance off the beaches and respond to requests for specific target destruction. Guadalcanal and Tulagi were of key importance and, although the fighting was bitter, at least the American ground forces did not have to worry about being attacked from the air. An immensely important objective was sited on Guadalcanal – an airfield the Americans re-named Henderson Field. It had been established by the Japanese army to carry out attacks on these very American naval and marine invasions. Once overrun, its main purpose was turned crucially against the Japanese war effort to become a base for B-29s within range of Japan.

This was a tactical pattern repeatedly carried out as the Allied forces implemented their island-hopping strategy. The larger and more severely fortified islands were bypassed whenever it made sense to do so. The islands were invested but no Allied troops assaulted them. Heavy casualties could be thus avoided, bottling the enemy up in their jungle-covered underground redouts, isolating and reducing them by air bombardment, naval blockade and starvation.

Such operations had to be achieved in the initial phases of the war without the protection of many heavy supporting naval units, as most of the US battleships and heavy cruisers were still undergoing repair or rebuild in Hawaii after the Pearl Harbour attack. It was warfare carried out by carriers escorted by lighter, surface-screening ships and by submarines. The thrust towards Japan concentrated on islands that looked, as with Tulagi, suitable for building air bases and supply dumps. The engagements involved uninterrupted air fighting and initially focused on Henderson Field.

The realization by the Japanese that repeated use of these methods would amount to a strategy that could turn things around for the Allies provoked a tremendous response. The Japanese ashore also knew that the Americans were aiming to get within bombing range of the homeland and fought with fierce determination. Their positions were carefully laid out, well entrenched and had concealed fire-points. It is estimated that there were around 30,000 Japanese troops in the battle and nearly all of them were killed. Victory came in July. While not of the same magnitude, US casualties were heavy and grievous.

The Allies had pushed back the Japanese perimeter further north away from Australia. Henderson Field was now close to operational. A vast civil engineering site it was still, but the foundations and basic infrastructure had already been laid by the Japanese themselves.

B-29 operations were close to becoming reality. This would provide air cover and resupply both General MacArthur's southern army engaging the Japanese in New Guinea, and secure Admiral Nimitz's southern flank. Nimitz commanded the force responsible for the island-hopping thrust. MacArthur would go on to clear New Guinea of the invading Japanese and eventually recover the Philippines, all the while pushing back the perimeter of the ironically named 'Japanese Co-Prosperity Sphere'. When Nimitz's forces secured the Marianas, the Japanese island homeland would at last fall within the radius of action of B-29 Superfortresses.

Guadalcanal is one of the biggest islands in the Solomons Group. The prolonged fighting which takes its name from that place was not so much a battle as a prolonged campaign lasting from August 1942 for six months. Such a timescale demanded that lines of resupply remained open. Offshore there was a continual naval battle as blockading naval units were involved trying to outdo each other in the interdiction of each other's supply lines. The US carrier planes achieved critical air superiority which meant that airborne logistics, a developing operational science, offered great opportunity and the Americans took it.

It was a critical factor. Air supply of armies in the field was necessary because much of this fighting took place in thick rain forest where there were few or no roads. It became standard practice in some areas. Allied armies further north, such as those committed to Burma (The Chindits) and Malaya (Force 136), were supplied almost entirely by air. Denied the air option, the Japanese logistic effort was by sea, which was vulnerable and met with limited success.

The naval battle to get supplies through inflicted heavy losses on the US Navy, but maximum effort was being achieved in ship building in the United States to replace those losses and this was unmatched by Japan. The factory battle, fought thousands of miles away, began to become outcome critical. The initial heavy losses of men in the United States forces brought a stateside response in the form of large-scale reinforcement and this too weighed the odds in favour of the Americans – Japan was unable to come close to matching it. The early augurs were suggesting a United States victory, but it was not to happen at any time soon.

The losses of men on both sides were grim with as many as 30,000 on the Japanese side, three-quarters of whom died from tropical disease and even starvation. Strategically, it stopped in its tracks any possibility of further advance towards Australia and at the end of Guadalcanal came the reacquisition of the Solomons themselves. The threat to Australia had been forestalled, as had the strategic ability to attack traffic on the east-west shipping routes in the South Pacific and across the Indian Ocean. The Coral Sea, Midway, and Guadalcanal taken together comprised a turning point in the Pacific War. The Japanese evacuated what was left of their forces in Guadalcanal. They were now strategically on the defensive.

By June 1944, US Marines and soldiers of the American Army were invading Saipan in the Mariana Islands. Saipan was picked as a base for B-29s, again because it placed the islands of the Japanese homeland within their radius of action. As these were amphibious operations, US Marines were the spearhead, and to ensure resupply for them and protection from attack by carrier-borne aircraft, there was yet another rolling naval battle going on out to sea.

Known as the Battle of the Philippine Sea, it lasted for over two days. It broke the back of the IJN's carrier might. The largest carrier-to-carrier battle so far, it enjoined twenty-four aircraft carriers from both sides and over 1,300 emplaned aircraft. It was a tour de force for the USN aircrew and their anti-aircraft gunners. The aircrew called it the 'Great Marianas Turkey Shoot', commemorating the imbalance of losses between the sides. The USN lost 123 planes.

The IJN lost around 600 plus three carriers and an oil tanker. The USN pilots overwhelmed the aerial opposition decisively using better thought-out combat tactics, battle deployment and having the advantage of experienced and battle-hardened aviators. There were also a lot of them.

The gunnery sailors had the same advantages plus one innovation that gave them a real edge – the proximity fused shell. Up to now shells had been detonated by contact – you had to hit what you were firing at. This was very difficult when engaging a fast-moving manoeuvring target from a heaving deck. Estimation of the ratio of hits achieved to shells fired ranged from hundreds to thousands to one. This was now improved by orders of magnitude.

While all this mayhem was raging above the waves, two USN submarines managed to get in close. They sank two of the Japanese carriers and made a crucial contribution to the outcome of the battle. The American carriers delivered unending waves of aircraft hoping to overwhelm the Japanese carriers by sheer relentless numbers. There was a big price to pay for this – how to recover them on return. Many of the returning aircraft ended up in a queue to land without the fuel to wait their turn; and it was getting dark. No less than eighty of them were lost, many forced to ditch. Some, but far from all the aircrew, were rescued.

The battle proved an act of grinding attrition, again not in itself a finality, but it set the scene for the Battle of Leyte Gulf four months later in October 1944. However, the Philippine Sea battle could fairly claim to have been the end of the IJN's ability or willingness to depend on further carrier war. Its few remaining fleet (strike) carriers stayed moored in port. This implied that the IJN had accepted that a strategic victory at sea was no longer a viable possibility, and its role now was the interdiction of the Allies' island-hopping invasions, using surface vessels, principally battleships, heavy cruisers, and fast torpedo boats, but also submarines. The next major reconquest attempted by the Americans was going to be the Philippines.

In the autumn of 1944, the US Navy and the Imperial Japanese Navy closed with each other at Leyte Gulf in the Philippines. The strategic importance of this contest to Japan was that the loss of the Philippines would cut off the home islands completely from the newly acquired resources of far Southeast Asia, including vital supplies of oil and rubber. They organised naval forces into the approaches from the north, south and west. The relief of the Philippines by the US commenced on the northeast island of Leyte. The first objective was to land and secure a beachhead, drive inland and establish a base. 130,000 American troops with thousands of tons of materiel were landed and a base established.

It was, however, vulnerable, being isolated and it was also near large Japanese forces. The IJN had long been expecting the invasion, had planned and prepared for it. Their plans had to be continuously modified as the Allied war efforts constantly neutralised and destroyed their military assets faster than they could be replaced. Cutting the sea lanes was critical to this process and the continual sea fighting was taking its toll.

The IJN's latest plan involved three naval thrusts taking place together, a northern, central and southern. They commenced execution of the plans, the three prongs to converge on Leyte Gulf. Most of Japan's naval resources were committed to this gigantic operation. It was fully understood that the Philippines were pivotal to Japan's ability to replenish its war effort but also to keeping the enemy at bay from the homeland. Losing Leyte Island meant losing the war. As a mark of desperation this was the first battle where Kamikaze attacks were employed, with the battle for Okinawa yet to come. They were a shock, but lethal as the attacks were, they came too late, and in too few numbers to affect the outcome of the battle or of the war.

Two patrolling USN submarines to the west of the islands detected part of the converging Japanese forces and sank two cruisers. More importantly, they signalled the position of part of the Japanese forces to the naval commanders – Admirals Kinkaid and Halsey. Halsey in the 3rd Fleet launched reconnaissance planes to get a clearer picture. The search planes found part of the IJN steaming directly east through the archipelago making for the San Bernardino Strait from where it would have been possible to turn direction and threaten Leyte Gulf. The US fleet carriers were ordered to launch strike planes. On 24 October 1944, the torpedo bombers, opposed only by anti-aircraft fire, located the massive 73,000 ton battleship *Musashi*, and made six attacks. Several of them hit home and eventually the great ship foundered. She and her sister ship *Yamato*, and toting nine 18-inch guns, were the biggest battleships ever built, yet she was sunk entirely by air attack. The IJN central force now turned back to avoid further destruction. It had been deterred from reaching Leyte.

The IJN southern force arrived at the Mindanao Sea and turned east to threaten Leyte Island through the Surigao Strait. Informed of this by intelligence reports, USN warships moved from the west to converge on Surigao using it as a huge gauntlet through which the enemy fleet would have to run.

Fast patrol torpedo (PT) boats went ahead – a courageous gambit given that the surprise and stealth on which they relied would be lost in the first minutes of engagement. Destroyers pushed west after them to picket the Strait and watch for submarine activity. Cruisers positioned next behind the destroyers. The final line comprised the battleships, all proudly bearing the names of American states, *California, Maryland, Tennessee, West Virginia*. This was an ambush in depth. It was also seen as a grudge match for Pearl Harbour by

American battleship crews. If the Japanese tried to force the passage, things could only get worse as they encountered increasingly heavy Allied units. Unaware, the combined Japanese force swept on towards them in the darkness.

It was midnight when the IJN radars detected the American fleet. Both sides lit the skies with searchlights and flares as the PT boats went all out, picking targets and firing torpedoes at them before wheeling about and fleeing. Their job was not quite finished. Getting close enough to launch a torpedo meant you had pinpointed the exact position of the enemy, and these reports were passed back to the heavy units of Admiral Kinkaid's 7th Fleet. By the time the IJN realised they had sailed into a carefully deployed trap, it was too late. They were constrained in manoeuvre by the shores of the Strait and funnelled towards the waiting Allied battleships' guns. Salvo after salvo was exchanged. The Japanese southern force, bottled up, took a severe mauling and was finished as a viable threat. Its casualties numbered around 5,000.

This, however, was not the only battle raging. The central Japanese task force, having reversed course, was now inside the San Bernardino Strait in the north of the archipelago. The USN units picketing this area were relatively light. The heaviest units were escort carriers. Their aircrafts' purpose (fighters and reconnaissance planes) was to defend their own units. They were incapable of attacking the enemy fleet itself.

In this engagement, the USN with light cruisers and destroyers was significantly outgunned by the IJN force with its cruisers and battleships. Destroyers and light cruisers taking on cruisers and battleships, including the *Yamato*, could not be considered desirable practice. The progress of this Japanese task force had to be challenged, however, because the guns of its twenty-two ships could bring catastrophe to the Leyte Island invasion landings now in full swing further south.

The US destroyers, not cowed by what they knew they faced, did not disappoint. They cut across and along the lines of battle laying smoke screens to rob the Japanese gun-layers of ability to judge visual range, then turned under the smoke to close and deliver torpedo attacks at the much larger ships. The outlook seemed grim indeed for the unarmoured destroyer force who were being savaged, but after sinking five ships, suddenly, inexplicably, the Japanese fleet turned away and broke off the engagement.

There was no time to reason why as shortly afterwards the position of the Japanese northern task force was deliberately given away by false transmissions, and that it was making all speed south. This force had originally been a feint to confuse Admiral Halsey and draw his forces away from Leyte. It succeeded with that part of its mission and Halsey did indeed turn his 7th Fleet away north from guarding Leyte, a decision that was acrimoniously debated subsequently.

The IJN northern force included four fleet carriers with their strike planes, along with battleships and heavy cruisers. In turning south, their feint phase now over, they knew they would have to fight Halsey's battle group and that in all probability their carriers would be the primary targets for strike planes from the American fleet carriers. The Japanese force had to be disrupted because the twenty-two ships of the group could bring havoc to the Leyte Island landings further south had they broken through.

The first strike was launched from the American fleet – 165 torpedo bombers, dive bombers and escort fighters. The primary defence for the Japanese ships was not now the fighters from escort carriers – too many of these had been irreplaceably lost – but reliance only on the batteries of anti-aircraft weapons, many more of which had been fitted to try to make good the loss. Japanese land-based

B-29 cockpit.

B-29s in olive green camouflage.

With a wingspan of 141 feet the B-29 was not the biggest of the war, but it was the most successful of the large aircraft.

B-29 sting in the tail.

Boeing B-29. (© *Alan Wilson/wikicommons*)

Three of a kind - B-17 Flying Fortress; B-29 Superfortress and B-52 Stratofortress.

Bombs Away!

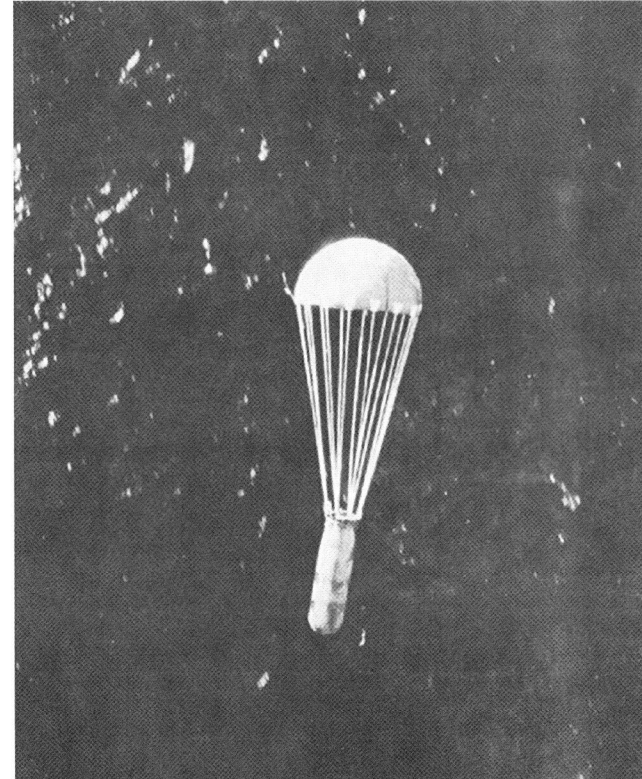

Aerial Mine Laying. This is a
1,000lb Mark 26 mine dropped
by a 313th Bomb Wing B-29
in 1945. Mines were dropped at
specified intervals by formations
of bombers, but to create a
minefield took a lot of skill from
the navigator and bombardier.

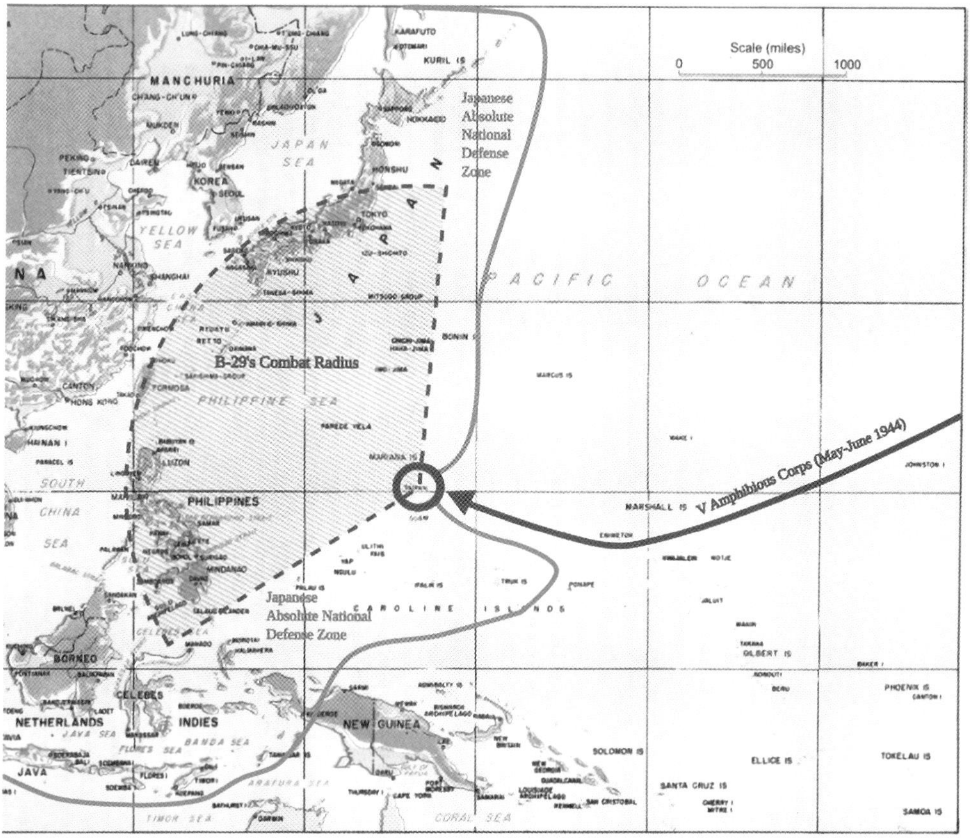

Map of B-29 range from Saipan. © Wtfiv/wikicommons

Front Crew –
Pilot, Bombardier
– Copilot

Flight Engineer's "office".

B-29 pair over Fuijiama.

P-51 Mustang escorting a B-29. The P-51 was the only single-engine fighter of the war with the range to be able to do this. Note the huge fuel drop tanks. This photograph might have been near base; on the outbound leg it would have been well above the bombers.

Surrender of Japan, Tokyo Bay, 2 September 1945: Representatives of the Empire of Japan on board USS Missouri (BB-63) during the surrender ceremonies.

bombers from Luzon lent heavy support and managed to set ablaze the USS light carrier *Princeton*.

At the finish the northern fleet, outnumbered and vulnerable against a foe that had achieved air superiority over them, went the same way as their two other task forces. The Imperial Japanese Navy lost twenty-six warships, and in a battle lasting only four days, one of the best navies in the world became a broken, spent force.

The island of Leyte was recaptured, the fighting ceasing by the end of the year with Leyte thereafter in America's possession. 12,000 Japanese sailors and airmen perished, four times as many as the USN. The aircraft losses were more even with the Japanese losing approximately 300 to the US Navy's 250. It is estimated that 65,000 Japanese soldiers died defending Leyte Island itself. More than 15,000 Americans were killed or wounded.

In January 1945, the US Army under General Douglas MacArthur invaded Luzon in the Philippines. It was a very large army and needed to be as it was about to attack a force of nearly 300,000 Japanese soldiers, as usual fully prepared and dug in.

It lasted for over two months and at the end of it there were over 10,000 dead, three times as many wounded on the Allied side and over a quarter of a million dead on the Japanese. Over half a million civilians perished including those during the Japanese occupation. The Philippines, however, were freed.

Chapter 7

Island Hopping

The choice to invade the Japanese-conquered islands and finally Japan itself by American troops had brought with it the absolute requirement of a critical reduction of the means of how the enemy might interdict the main thrust. Their capital ships had to be sunk and their navy critically enfeebled. This was achieved.

A second necessity was the huge effort to plan and equip for invading islands in the western Pacific. This was the 'Island Hopping' plan. The thrust had to be aimed closer and closer to the Japanese mainland. This could not be the re-conquest of a narrow corridor of stepping stones, because such a progression would be vulnerable to flank attack, now and always afterwards. The swathe had to be broadly based, literally, with mutually supporting general thrusts and defendable flanks. It formed a fearful prospect in the minds of US policy makers and planners.

The Japanese soldier had been inured to believe that the worst thing of all was disgrace, and, above all things, surrender was disgraceful. Fighting to the death was the only honourable option. It was reinforced by iron military discipline. Like the Nazis, they were viciously nationalistic and regarded other nationalities as sub-human, to be dealt with ruthlessly and without pity. They were ordered never to surrender but, on the assumption that they were going to die, their supreme duty was to kill as many American soldiers as they could before they met their own fate.

They commonly complied with this code. This meant that any advance by American forces would be at great cost in lives and wounded. Doctrine at the time often assumed offence-defence ratios in the order of five to one; in other words, to overrun a unit in a prepared defensive position required at least five times as many troops as the defenders. The exact ratio was variously debated but, in any case, estimates in millions of casualties to invade and conquer the Japanese homeland were given credence.

In the autumn of 1944, the US Navy and the Imperial Japanese Navy closed within strike range of each other at Leyte Gulf in the Philippines. This was the first battle where Kamikaze attacks were employed, but by no means the last. They were a huge shock to the American sailors and a headache for the Admirals commanding them, but it did not affect the outcome. Arguably the biggest carrier battle in history, it marked the end for the Japanese navy, who were disrupted as a viable strategic threat. In the battle ashore, 65,000 Japanese soldiers died, and 15,000 Americans were killed or wounded.

In January 1945, the Army under General Douglas MacArthur invaded Luzon in the Philippines. It lasted for over two months and at the end of it there were probably over three-quarters of a million killed including civilians.

A month later, in February, a small volcanic island – Iwo Jima – was attacked. The operation was intended to secure this barren place to build further runways for B-29 missions to bomb the Japanese mainland directly and return. Its proximity was sufficient for the bombers to carry full bombloads. More of the same – the Japanese were skilfully entrenched. After over a month of rabid fighting the enemy was overcome but at the cost of 7,000 dead, mostly Marines. 24,000 were wounded.

Of the Japanese force, only about 1,000 were captured, but the rest – 20,000 – were killed or committed suicide. Iwo Jima was halfway between Saipan in the Marianas, where the main B-29 base was to be situated, and Tokyo on the main Japanese island of Honshu. The round trip from Saipan to Tokyo and back was 3,000 miles and it was a great comfort to the crews to know that in the event of an aircraft emergency anywhere on the trip, especially battle damage going critical on the return leg, there was a relief landing ground available half-way home.

The number of dead injured or missing had mounted, battle by battle, island by island. The tallies were inexact, no doubt, but even in those times of statistical uncertainty some things must have been evident. Experience had shown that while American losses might measure in thousands, Japanese losses might measure in tens of thousands, and with civilian losses, were they unfortunate enough to get trapped between the two warring sides, could reach hundreds of thousands. It was assumed that it would get worse the closer the fighting came to the Japanese mainland.

This became a nightmare scenario when attempting to predict the death and casualty rates that would result from an actual invasion of Japan and fighting through Japan, until it was exhausted of all resource. It was also to say nothing of Japanese military casualties and those of the civil population. No doubt, as is expected in democracy, there was a spread of opinion between the optimistic and the pessimistic, but two months later there came the final heave 350 miles from Japan, and this confirmed the worst fears. Okinawa was the choice for the invasion of Japan, but first it had to be invaded, secured, and readied for the role. Just when everyone hoped it couldn't get worse, it did.

Okinawa took nearly three months of the most monstrous fighting to quell it. It was everything already encountered, but bigger and more formidable than predicted. American troops, Marines and Army, fought for every yard against an enemy that was not only entrenched but living and hiding underground in interconnecting tunnels and chambers. These not only provided shelter and protection but enabled troops to rest out of the weather, get a night's sleep, move, regroup and reinforce without danger of air or ground attack as they did so. Access to the tunnel systems was difficult as they had been carefully concealed. The whole set up was a massive ambush.

At the end of an agonising experience for the troops on both sides, American troops and naval personnel won the day but not before 12,000 were dead or unaccounted on the American side, with the wounded at 36,000. The Japanese lost 70,000 soldiers. The number of the civilian population killed is incalculable with any accuracy but numbers of between 100,000 and 150,000 have been estimated. This all added to the trepidation about invasion of Japan itself and the favouring of alternatives.

While the suicidal fighting determination of the Japanese soldier had been experienced in many battles, something had happened in mid-1944 back in Saipan that was an even more shocking revelation. As the US Marines and Army ground their way across the island, the incumbent population started to kill themselves in large numbers! Whether this was because Americans had been demonised by Japanese propaganda, or whether it was inspired by the Bushido code, or by extreme nationalism, was a hugely important quandary. Possibly it was a mix of all three. Bushido – the 'Way of the Warrior' would not have been generally applicable to civilians, but when the news of mass suicides reached Japan, the government attempted to harness it by declaring those who had taken their own lives as heroic and urged the whole population of Japan to be prepared to do the same thing if the Americans invaded the homeland.

How could such a situation have come about? The Japanese Bushido code was widely referenced because the Japanese military under the emperor, whom they regarded as a god, had an iron grip on political power in the country. In so far as those with political power can decide, even dictate the behaviours and value codes of those they rule, it is understandable that this thinking and example would have affected the values of the Japanese people. The Kamikaze pilot was the highest modern manifestation of the true Samurai warrior and deeply admired. This attitude of mind – death before surrender – death before dishonour – had massive prejudicial consequences when it came to putting an end to the war.

Taking the other adversary, the American attitude towards war was also absolutist, a tradition having grown from historical experience. A war, once started, could only be stopped by the unconditional surrender of the enemy. Their strategic determination was embedded in beliefs grounded in liberal democratic values but was more optimistic than the glowering defiance of the Japanese. The President, as Supreme Commander, his political staff and advisors, the Generals and Admirals to whom operations would be delegated, always needed to work out the best way to win any phase within the context of final total victory; not the honourable way to lose. These two mind sets had determination in common but, in terms of ways to end the war as soon as possible, they were mutually incompatible. One demanded unconditional surrender; the other was committed to refuse it utterly. After Pearl Harbour, the war had become a war of values, a fight to the finish, and the casualties would continue to be enormous and increasing, both in military and civilian terms. Critically, the American government was asking the question – what *will* make them surrender unconditionally? Would anything?

Chapter 8

The Boeing B-29 Superfortress

In the early days of the USAAF's attempt at daylight bombing in Europe, the losses to men and aircraft were eventually overcome, but it was a close-run thing. Inevitably, those involved at the sharp end formed ideas of what they would have done differently to improve their tactics and weaponry.

In Europe, the strategic air battle had been fought over a land mass. Involvement with an ocean had indeed been strategic – operating and protecting the logistical flow of materiel across the North Atlantic – but it had been fought and won by others. The interruptions to the flow of equipment and supplies were real and heart-rending, but the navies of the two Allied protagonists pressed home their efforts, and, eventually, diminished the sinkings of supply ships to a survivable level. The U-boats were eventually beaten, mainly by deep-sea, fleet destroyers and maritime patrol aircraft such as the British Short Sunderland and the American Consolidated Liberator.

With their increasing ranges, they had finally closed the 'Mid Atlantic Gap'. This was the vast strip of sea running north-south in the mid North Atlantic out of the range of maritime bombers flying from both Britain and the United States. It had been a safe haven for U-boats, which could travel on the surface unchallenged while all the time re-charging batteries and air supplies ready for the next opportunity to submerge, attack and sink shipping. The U-boat *(Unterseeboot)*, unlike modern submarines, was not a vessel that spent most of its life cruising silently below the waves. In fact, these craft spent most of their time on the surface, either out of reach, or at night where they were more difficult to spot. Surfaced, their vulnerability increased hugely. Night cruising was an imperfect answer as a surfaced craft, even at conning-tower depth, could still be picked up by a patrol aircraft's search radar and attacked with bombs or depth charges. In the Mid-Atlantic Gap, they had a respite until increasing air patrol ranges from both the British and the American coasts squeezed it out of existence. The next strategic air battles would be fought over and around the Pacific Ocean but, as one American Admiral drily remarked, the North Atlantic was, 'a duck-pond compared with the Pacific'. The problems encountered in Europe would be encountered over the Pacific, but they would increase by an order of magnitude.

The B-29's development was born out of necessity during World War II, when the US Army Air Forces needed a long-range bomber that could fly higher, faster, and further than existing heavy bombers. It had the Pacific theatre in mind. In 1939, the Army Air Force issued a requirement for a bomber with a range of 5,000 miles and capable of carrying a bombload of 20,000lb.

Such a machine would be in a class of its own – incomparable with anything that existed. Boeing, along with other manufacturers, submitted designs, and the Boeing Model 345 was chosen. The B-29 'Superfortress' as it became known, was a step-change in bomber technology. It could go high, having a service ceiling of nearly 32,000ft enabled by its powerful 2,200-horsepower (hp), twin-banked, radial engines, the most powerful piston aero-engine in the entire war. It had a long wingspan of 140ft. The wings had a high aspect ratio – they were long in relation to the chord length (width across the wing). This reduced the drag-inducing vortices at its wingtips, which not only increased its height capability but, critically, its range performance. It was equipped with pressurized crew compartments, which allowed the crew to fly at high altitudes in relative comfort—a significant innovation given that all other bombers of the time were unpressurized, leaving crews exposed to freezing temperatures and thin air at high altitudes. The high-altitude capability was critical for avoiding enemy fighters and anti-aircraft fire.

The new, big Boeing continued the tradition that heavy bombers of the day must have defensive guns, but they were unlike anything before. Some of its turrets were not manned, the guns being aimed and fired from remote positions assisted by early analogue computers. This was a world far removed from that experienced by B-17 Fortress gunners where the firing of defensive machine guns was up close and personal. There was no more shooting out of open hatches while the gunners were trying to cope with the miserable distractions of frostbite and altitude sickness, and no more hanging upside down in ball turrets. The gunners sat at warm stations, in an atmosphere pressurized equivalent to below 10,000ft where they didn't even need the oxygen available from their breathing equipment if they chose not to use it. They could aim and fire turret guns singly or in multiples from within the fuselage.

The engine chosen to power the new Boeing was the Wright R-3350 radial comprising eighteen cylinders arranged in two banks, one behind the other. Each was twin-supercharged, giving a power output of about 2,200hp on introduction, but which rose to over 3,500hp as the engine was developed with use, primarily by increased supercharging pressures.

The need for such an aircraft had been well-anticipated and, unlike the B-17 Fortress, where the development process did not have such a deliberate feel about it, got through prototype to commencement of production stage by 1943. The cooling of the rear banks of cylinders, a known problem with this engine lay-out, duly did cause problems, but that had a lot of attention paid to it. However, it also had another latent problem – the malfunctioning of the engine cowling flaps. These flaps were used to increase cooling airflow over the engines but would sometimes fall open causing a great deal of asymmetric drag. If the failed engine was one of the two outers, the aircraft would be very difficult to fly straight and level in this condition. The additional drag was also sufficient to slow the aircraft, sometimes dangerously close to stalling speed, and always curtailing the aircraft's range capability. Many were reputed lost but that did not deter its commanders. The aircraft continued in service. It had a mission to fulfil that could shorten the war, which no other aircraft could do, and with or without flaws, it was going to do it.

It had a maximum take-off weight of 141,000lb, which dwarfed its predecessor B-17. Its four Wright radials gave the bomber a maximum speed of 350mph. The B-29's service ceiling of (31,200 ft), allowed it to fly above most of the weather. It could indeed carry up to 20,000lb of bombs, depending on the mission and fuel load. The crew consisted of up to eleven men.

The B-29 has been described as a 'game-changer'. It would be more accurate to say that its arrival was a 'game winner'. The essentials of the game were the same – strategic air supremacy – but the game was now vastly bigger. Its designed range of 5,000 miles would enable it to attack the Japanese home islands from the Pacific Ocean. It implied establishing operating bases within a 2,000 mile arc, the extremity of a radius of action enabling the aircraft to recover to their launch bases. Recovery to a developed and well supplied base airfield was important because these were complicated new-technology machines. They were also the most expensive aircraft to date. They required huge amounts of replenishment fuel and weapons as well as unprecedented levels and standards of in-field engineering facilities. They needed the security of protection troops, fighter cover and naval patrols, civil engineering support and hospital facilities to care for the wounded that would inevitably result from operating against a determined enemy.

While no-one disputed that these machines were a brilliant incorporation of so many innovations, some of the most important things had not changed. Multi-engine aircraft presented an intriguing option – to shut the failed engine down and carry on regardless. If the aircraft was lightly loaded (bombs could be jettisoned) and in the cruise at altitude this was possible. Executed successfully, it could deliver a safe outcome, getting the aircraft safely on the ground. A bomber on a take-off role at the beginning of a sortie was none of those things. It would be heavily loaded, seriously overloaded by later standards, with fuel and high explosive. The fuel was petrol or gasoline – a spirit with a low flashpoint that could be ignited by a mere spark. The record-breaking bombload had to be handled with extreme care with absolutely no shocks to the system.

On take-off therefore, every ounce of power was demanded from the engines to accelerate the B-29 from stationary to the rotate speed, nose lifted and airborne. The risk did not stop there but continued until the wheels had been retracted, the flaps raised, both to reduce drag and increase speed, and the aircraft settled into a safe climb to get it away from the ground as quickly as possible. The engines would then be throttled back to 'max continuous' power to reduce the stress on them and therefore the odds that something would fail. Should an engine fail on a full load take-off, the take-off would have to be aborted – there would be insufficient power available on the remaining three engines. Now everything depended on the effectiveness of the brakes and the robustness of the undercarriage not to collapse. If it did so it was the worst. The propellors would contact the ground, bending back and shock-stopping the engines, which disrupted and produced an instant high risk of fire. As if that was not enough, the great behemoth was now skidding along on its belly, the bomb doors alone standing between the crew and disaster.

The crews of aircraft that did get airborne still had much to do and many more hazards to survive. The sortie, or 'mission', involved flying thousands of miles over the open ocean with little or often nothing available for a bomber that had developed a fault requiring a landing as soon as possible. 'Soon' was generally not possible. This danger abated to a degree as closer islands such as Okinawa and Iwo Jima were wrested back from Japanese control, enabling the Navy Seabee Battalions to construct airfields closer to the Japanese home islands. All these substantial challenges had to be overcome successfully by the crew – and so far they might not have encountered even a single fighter aircraft.

The Second World War was a time of exploration of the unknown, requiring new technologies to overcome the ensuing problems. One such problem emerged as fighter aircraft flew at increasing speeds. Pilots became aware that this could entail a large and sudden increase in propellor noise. Investigation showed that this was due to the tips of the propellor achieving a rotational velocity of close to supersonic speed and shockwaves.

Potentially destructive, this was countered by innovations such as squaring off the tips to make the propeller blades shorter or reducing rotational velocity while increasing pitch settings to maintain thrust values. By the end of the war, aircraft with jet engines dispensed with problematic propellors but they were insufficiently numerous to affect the outcome of the war. They did, however, give an early indication of which way aero-engine development would go in the post-war era. Aviation was entering the age of the jet. The B-29 also made such contributions. Able to reach and cruise close to the stratosphere, it regularly experienced winds of very high velocity and this had to be dealt with to avoid compromising accurate navigation. It could also seriously detract from the accuracy of bomb-aiming. It became known as the 'Jet Stream' and with increasing understanding became a normal part of long-range flight-planning, both military and civil. Aircrew learned to predict it, to deal with it and to be comfortable with it. The post-war civil airliner variant of the Superfortress was named the Stratocruiser.

Island-hopping became the name of the strategic range game, and the initial bases secured were on islands that included Guam, Saipan and Tinian from the start. They were close enough to bring the four major islands of the Japanese homeland within their striking range – Hokkaido, Kyushu, Shikoku and most of all, the main island of Honshu. Herculean efforts were made to ensure that adequate logistic and support facilities for the aeroplanes were set up prior to the arrival of the bombers and their crews.

In England during the European campaign, large numbers of civil engineering projects to produce big airfields could be delegated to a developed and capable British civil engineering industry, such as John Laing Ltd, which built Thorpe Abbots in Norfolk, England, home of the US Army 8th Air Force 100th Bomb Group.

The industry took on and completed the task of producing over fifty bomber airfields in record time. There was no such possibility in the far reaches of the Pacific Ocean. Everything had to be done from scratch by the military authorities themselves using recently formed Naval Construction Battalions or Seabees. They had been formed in 1943 in anticipation of this critical need in the Pacific and rose well to the task. The ability to take on civil engineering projects of this size made possible the strategic air campaign that was to prove a decisive option shortly afterwards.

Chapter 9

Strategic Bombing

The bombing of Japan was the culmination of a campaign that commenced months before and which had to include an intense naval phase to defeat the Imperial Japanese Navy. This was to ensure that there could be no sea-based interdiction of the long Allied supply lines essential to support what would have to be a massive air campaign. It was followed by the island-hopping reconquest of the Pacific islands, the most important strategic objective of which was to enable airfields to be constructed close enough to Japan to put it within the radius of strike of the B-29 Superfortress.

The Superfortress was the replacement for the B-17 Fortress. The B-17 had fought the strategic campaign successfully in Europe, albeit at great cost in men and machines, but would have been entirely inadequate for the Pacific War with the greatly increased distances involved. The Allied forces were already flying air raids attacking targets in China and Southeast Asia, principally using the Consolidated B-24 Liberator. As the B-29s started to arrive they joined this effort as part of working up.

The early results were poor. The B-29 crews were still bedding in with their new charges and at the limit of their capabilities even on a good-weather day. Many days were not good-weather days. Night flying was tried but rejected by General 'Hap' Arnold, a veteran commander of the European war against Germany and Commanding Officer of the newly formed 20th Air Force. He stopped it on a point of doctrine. He was an impressive commander. However, he harboured a visceral rejection of night bombing.

He had developed a warm friendship with Air Chief Marshal Sir Arthur Harris, commander of RAF Bomber Command. Harris took the opposite view – his strategic heavy bombers sortied mostly at night, ultimately with critical effect on the war in Europe. He attempted to persuade Arnold, but failed to do so. As he had with the B-17 Fortress in Europe, General Arnold insisted that his bombers in the Pacific had to be able to attack targets from high level in broad daylight, where they would have a height and sight advantage, as well as the critical immunity from anti-aircraft guns.

On his orders, night trials ceased. Tactics reverted to close formation flying providing mutual protection due to the concentration of a high number of guns carried by the bombers. It was history repeating itself. The assumptions seemed to be that the tactics in Europe had been right in principle but the planes, disappointingly, had not been up to it. There had been far more to it than that, but in this Pacific war there was hope that in the B-29 they would be flying an aircraft that was. But cloud is cloud, and fog is fog, no matter where it is located and more hard lessons had to be learned. As had been the standard procedure in Europe, the B-29s were required initially to use the same tactics as had been used by the B-17 Fortresses in that campaign and attacked using daylight precision bombing. But the weather over Japan was as bad and worse than over Europe.

In one of the first operations, 100 B-29s were to be accompanied by squadrons of B-24 Liberators to add further bombload. The briefing was over-crowded and filled with cigarette smoke. Their base was in China. The targets were in Bangkok. As dawn broke, the operation's designated airfields streamed forth hundreds of air crew, throwing away cigarette butts and putting in chewing gum.

The giants stood before them, wings slightly drooping, dazzling silver, menacing, even while silent. The groundcrew saluted in their usual nonchalant fashion. The crew hauled themselves into various entry points, turned right or left, settled themselves into their seats and strapped in. The weather was abysmal. The Bangkok area, where the targets were situated, was subject to the Monsoon, which filled the skies with huge cumulo-nimbus clouds and heavy precipitation. At these latitudes the tropopause, the boundary layer between the troposphere and the stratosphere and the vertical limit of weather, was at around 40,000ft, too high, even for the B-29, to climb over it. The savvy B-24 Liberator commanders cancelled the mission early.

A B-29 navigator, listening to local air traffic radio exchanges, was suddenly startled by a transmission from Operations. It told him that the three squadrons of Consolidated B-24 Liberators were to shut down and abort the mission. The B-24 crews had gratefully complied. The Liberators were going nowhere today. He reported it to the captain of his own aircraft,

'Colonel – the B-24s have scrubbed.'

There was moment of silence. Then the Colonel, who was also to lead the formation, said,

'Well, we are B-29s son, and the whole world's watching. Engineer – tell me when we are ready.'

The radio operator called group check in, and one by one, seven squadrons checked in ready to roll. The formation boss gave the controls to his co-pilot and waved chocks away. He spread his fingers and thumb wide to push the four throttles gently forward. The noise level from the four Cyclones, a loud pulsing growl, rose to a business-like roar and the B-29 vibrated and started, very slowly, to move. The ground sergeant glanced up at the sky in disbelief, stood to attention and, unusually, saluted crisply. The group commander noted this somewhat sourly and returned the compliment.

The giant taxied on towards the take off point with the flight engineer scrutinizing his instruments. The four engines passed the testing routines, temperatures and pressures, magneto drops, propellor pitches to fully fine and the flaps were selected to the take-off setting as the plane was turned slowly onto the runway heading,

'We are cleared for take-off.'

The giant roared, lurched forward and in a few seconds was thundering down the runway, faster and faster, while the non-handling pilot scanned the engine gauges for any sign of deviation that might mean an abort.

'Rotate!'

The huge, segmented plexiglass nose rose up majestically. The rate of climb and descent indicator (RCDI) duly obliged by indicating a rate of climb. The handling pilot selected a nose up climb attitude on his artificial horizon (AI) and started a radial scan of the instruments on the blind-flying panel. The commander selected wheels up, flaps up, paused, then eased back the throttles to max-continuous rpm on all engines. He didn't have time to synchronize them right now – he would do that later. He listened out on radio to local control as each of the following aircraft called 'Airborne'.

He was now in control of the form-up and the aircraft broke cloud at 8,000ft. The following squadrons knew what to look for and every minute brought more and more bombers into a huge skein behind him. After half an hour, the lead aircraft had thirty bombers on his tail still climbing upwards through 15,000ft. There were more to join up, but the later take-offs, looking up as they broke cloud, would see the stream and be able to join up at their allocated station in the great formation. The target seemed, and was, a long way from home base.

The navigator, gathering actual wind and temperature data during this first phase, calculated an initial compass heading for the pilot to steer. Then as now, banter was important to crew morale.

'What heading, Nav?'

'Steer 138 degrees, Sir.'

'Sounds suspiciously precise.'

'Sir, we used to head 138 degrees a lot when we were training in Kansas. It always seemed to work!'

'Well, thank-you Lieutenant. That fills me with confidence.'

'You're very welcome, Colonel.'

The bombing group was now encountering reduced visibility as they continued to climb and it took a lot of concentration to form up. While most did so, no less than fourteen lost contact and aborted. With the deteriorating flight conditions, slowly, and despite the best efforts of the pilots, the great formation lost co-ordination. Pressing on for significant chunks of time the handling pilots would lose sight of other members of the formation and then were obliged to stick to the next aircraft, usually for long periods. It was never possible to predict what would present itself when eventually they flew into clear sky. An increasing number found themselves left to their own devices.

Many aircraft did not locate the target at all. The target was attacked essentially by singleton aircraft loitering over the target area (never a good idea) trying to find something worth bombing. They then had to position the bomber at the right distance out, pointing in the right direction, for a run-in to give their computerised bombsites a chance to acquire the target. Alternatively, they could be blessed with a clear stretch of sky and spot something that looked worth attacking, and bank towards it. Once the bombardier had confirmed he knew which thing on the ground he was ordered to aim at, up to 30,000ft below, he then had to 'con' the handling pilot on to it and drop the bombs by eye and judgement.

The 20thAir Force in Asia had one big blessing that the 8th USAAC did not have in the skies over Europe – flak and fighter opposition were light or non-existent. The formation did not meet the fighter or anti-aircraft opposition expected. Japanese strategy for protecting the homeland from aerial attack relied on their conquest of surrounding countries to put their homeland beyond the range of land-based aircraft. They did not prepare seriously against air attack until it was too late. The B-29s, operating from the Mariana Islands, eventually made nonsense of that assumption. Late on parade, Japanese fighter pilots were neither adequately trained nor battle hardened. Critically, ground co-ordination, which had acted as force multipliers for the RAF in the Battle of Britain and for the Luftwaffe in the European war, proved poor. The bomber squadrons incurred losses, but nothing comparable with those suffered by the 8th USAAC over Germany.

On the way back to base, they ran into thunderstorms. Forty aircraft, now mostly operating as singletons, picked themselves diversions as weather back at base got worse. Most of them ended up safely on the ground but at airfields scattered all over China. Three crashed in the process of diversion and one other did make it back to base but crashed on landing. Five aircraft were lost in the raid and seventeen crew were killed or unaccounted for. Post-raid reconnaissance showed no significant damage had been achieved. It was claimed as a success, but it must have been judged against a very low criterion. More likely, it had to be presented as a success for reasons of general morale and impressions given to Capitol Hill. As the war progressed, however, B-29 crews' experience accumulated, and results improved.

Raiding occupied territory was one thing but did little to bring the Pacific War nearer to a close. Only attacking the Japanese home islands was going to do that. The first attempt, in June 1944, was again launched from China involving a round-trip sortie of around 3,000 miles. Nearly seventy bombers took off but only just over half of them attacked the target area. There was an underlying problem. Both General Arnold and General LeMay were driven to complain that their success was being compromised by the problems of logistical resupply, which had to fly in everything from the west over the Himalayas, known to aircrew as 'The Hump'. To aviate safely over or through the highest mountain range in the world took careful flying and lots of fuel, which in turn reduced payloads considerably, demanding more flights, more time and more risks.

A further significant hindrance to success was that, to reach targets in Japan from these mainland bases, it was necessary to carry extra fuel, which, as noted, reduced bombload. That was anathema to Arnold and particularly to LeMay. There was nothing for it but to wait and hope that all the lives, treasury and time being invested in Admiral Nimitz's central Pacific thrust would deliver bases close enough to Japan to raid the home islands using B-29s with maximum bombloads and brimming with fuel.

Eventually this became a reality. The retaking of the Marianas made it possible to move B-29s to operate out of Tinian and Guam and of course hugely improved the logistical possibilities – islands can be supplied by freight ships and fuel tankers. Yet the first attempt had to wait until the end of that year. The first such raid was by a small force of eighty-eight planes and unsurprisingly they selected Tokyo as the target for maximum shock. Conditions were fair, but hits on the target were sparse. More flying experience was required and that, at least, was not going to be in short supply.

General Curtis LeMay was not a man to change his mind easily. He had supreme confidence that strategic bombing could be shaped to win wars, and a conviction that the formula championed by the air force like-minders, 'the Bomber Mafia', was right. He was also convinced that it had to be applied with pitiless determination and persistence to make it work. He was critical and sceptical about the need for fighter escorts, even in the form of the North American P-51 Mustang. The P-51 fighter, with its single-engine agility and incomparable range performance had eventually saved the 'Bombers Alone' doctrine and possibly the careers of its advocates from failure in Europe by drastically reducing the unsupportable losses in bomber aircraft being sustained by the USAAF. LeMay believed that, to win you could not be half-hearted about the task but would be required to apply the doctrine to the maximum possible. If precision bombing against industrial targets to prevent collateral damage was not a practical proposition, then mass area attacks on populated areas had to be used instead.

The emphasis moved from minimizing to maximizing the killing of populations and the infrastructures that supported them, in particular housing. Strategic precision bombing did continue but was greatly reduced and such crews were ordered to attack at low level during the daytime when target areas had been softened by raids during previous nights. Jointly these raids destroyed about 45% of Japan's biggest industrial urban areas. LeMay selected targets in order of size. Tokyo was the prime target as the biggest and the capital. Nagoya and Osaka were also high on the list. In a fire raid on the city of Kobe half the industrial sites were destroyed including a valuable shipyard with its dock facilities. The same month, Tokyo had the full fury of this new tactic meted out to it. In a maximum effort over a two-week period, 16 square miles were obliterated and an estimated 100,000 people died. The fearsome killer was the fire storm.

Incendiary, or fire-bombing, was not an innovation, but a tactic that had already been adopted during 1944 by RAF Bomber Command in attacks on cities such as Hamburg and Dresden. In its war with Germany going back five years, Air Marshal Sir Arthur Harris had reached the conclusion that with such targets incendiary weapons could be far more lethal than high explosive. An explosive bomb would damage a limited area. In contrast, incendiary bombs didn't try to knock anything down, but simply started fires. Once fires had been established however, they were self-sustaining, would eventually join up into a larger fire and then, a vast conflagration and stoked by winds, would indeed spread like the proverbial wildfire. Injecting so much energy into the atmosphere produces superheated air which rises rapidly, pulling in more oxygenated air from below and producing a cyclic inferno. The resulting winds could reach hurricane strength over a very large area. It is not possible to survive this horror, even underground, where people asphyxiated. In the days of long continuous attacks on Hamburg even the Elbe River, under a skim of oil, caught fire and desperate swimmers perished. In Tokyo it was reported that the river boiled. The Tokyo raids held the record as the most destructive ever, and the deadliest in terms of lives lost. Even the atomic raids that were to follow did not surpass it.

Only twenty-two B-29s failed to return from this group of raids. This was in stark contrast to the grievous losses suffered by their predecessors in the European campaign, which measured in hundreds of aircraft and thousands of aircrew. As the effects bit, so LeMay's force numbers grew to 600 aircraft. The assumption that the limits of the Japanese empire were so far-flung that the homeland could never be bombed and therefore required no powerful fighter defence, was wrecked as surely as its cities.

LeMay had been promoted to command the 21st Bomber Command in attacks on the Japanese homeland. He had taken over from General 'Hap' Arnold. While he proved rigid on the strategic points, in this campaign he proved ready to adjust tactics if things went wrong enough. He cannot have wished to repeat the cost in planes and lives he had experienced in Europe and where he himself had made a point of flying and leading from the front. So, when early results proved discouraging, he did something he had flatly refused to do in Europe. He rescinded the high-level, daylight precision bombing order and switched to medium-level night area bombing.

Cities were big targets and were impossible to hide even in night-time. Descending the attack level from above 30,000ft to below 7,000ft increased the chances of seeing the ground, but in any case, area bombing did not call for the pin-point navigation and spot-on bomb releases required of precision targets such as a factory. Everything was a target including residential areas, so the task for bomber crews moved from requiring a high degree of skill and luck and was rendered relatively simple. Navigation leaders could be tasked to lead in formations and act as on-board 'pathfinders'.

Incendiary weapons, a combination of a gelling agent and petroleum, produced an instant local inferno. It was later named Napalm. They were terrible in their effect, the first successful mass fire raids taking place in February 1945 on the city of Kobe. Japanese builders used highly flammable materials to build such as wood and even paper. The Japanese authorities, when they had no choice but to confront this disastrously complacent weakness, attempted to ameliorate the danger by opening firebreaks within their cities where the buildings were crammed together. This involved a vast demolition operation. They were destroying their own buildings, adding hugely to the destruction inflicted by their enemy. More than half a million of their own dwellings were destroyed in this way and a commensurate number of citizen workers and their families rendered homeless.

Because of the paucity of fighter opposition, B-29 losses were persistently low. This, combined with the impressive replacement rates by Boeing and other supporting US companies, LeMay's force numbers, having climbed to around 600, remained there. This left more than enough for him to turn his attention to second-sized cities and their manufacturing infrastructures. Eventually, LeMay, like Harris, reported that he was running out of worthwhile targets.

The destruction rapidly disrupted the fabric of the Japanese state and its economy. Estimates of the total number of deaths overall remain moot and may never be settled but there is no doubt it was cataclysmic. Some post hoc analysis concluded that this was the juncture where it became clear to many Japanese that Japan was now bound to lose the war and must surrender to limit the horror of such onslaught. However, the governance of Japan remained with the military faction, whose thinking was still conditioned by the values of Bushido and which implied a fight to the absolute finish and a glorious death for the entire nation. For this reason, though suing for surrender terms was now contemplated in Japan by many, its implementation was slow in becoming evident to their enemies. Given the American attitudes towards the conclusion of wars – unconditional surrender – this tardiness and indecision was to have horrific consequences.

LeMay was not just encouraged by the the effectiveness of fire raids. They convinced him that while the stated objective was to smash as much as possible of the enabling infrastructure that would enable the Japanese people to resist an invasion by American troops, given a free hand, strategic bombing alone could drive the Japanese to unconditional surrender. There was growing political support in the US too for bombing Japan with B-29s. This proved important in preventing moral arguments against mass bombing from gaining critical traction. President Roosevelt had decided to stand for President for a third time. He considered that to be associated with a war-winning strategy would increase his chances at the polls.

By now, other driving factors were about to come into play. The Soviet Union's non-aggression pact with Japan expired leaving that country free to join the war against them. And the Manhattan Project was soon to deliver for operational use two viable forms of atomic weapon. These offered two more strategic options, but whatever happened now, there would be no respite for the B-29.

Chapter 10

A Surfeit of Options

The main formations the US Navy had deployed throughout the far reaches of the Pacific and fought sea battle after sea battle to land and to keep secure the island-hopping army soldiers and marines in their mass assaults on the island redouts of the newly conquered Japanese empire. The objective, to capture islands that were both suitable for airfield construction and close enough to the enemy homeland to be used as bases for the Boeing B-29 Superfortress squadrons, had been achieved. Thereafter, the giant bombers had brought devastation to industrial and population centres of Japan.

It was anticipated that the ability of Japan to continue to wage war would be diminished to the point that surrender would become inevitable. This was the central strategy of the Pacific war, but many began to worry that a Japanese surrender was an assumption, not an inevitable fact. Japanese radio had praised the mass suicides of civilians during the US conquest of Saipan as heroic. It urged its population at home to be prepared to do the same thing. This would have been intercepted by USN Signals Intelligence Service.

What if the Japanese government, dominated still by the military faction, refused to surrender? It had become a credible possibility and would mean the Japanese islands would have to be invaded against an enemy determined to fight to the finish. This in turn would involve further huge losses of life of Allied servicemen and further vast expenditure of treasury to fund it. It would also take much more time, measured in many months.

This was not a possibility that anyone wished to entertain, especially the leaders of the democratic powers, the representatives of millions of their people, weary and distressed by so long and so vast a war. And there were elections looming. There is no doubt that these dire possibilities had a profound effect on the US government and its allies. This was to drive a need to consider options other than an invasion of the Japanese islands for the ending of the war. Too much more time; too much more treasury; too many more lives.

One important aspect of the invasion strategy was the proposed entry of Soviet Russia into the war to attack Japanese-conquered territory from the north on the mainland. Even in dire time of global war, the Russians had been punctilious about not breaking the non-aggression pact that existed between the Soviet Union, an Ally, and the Imperial Japanese Empire, an Axis power. This complicated things. On the expiry of the non-aggression pact, the Soviet Union did declare war on Japan. They commenced invasion operations in Manchuria. This would have been an enormous shock to the Japanese, especially after the Soviet rebuff of their request to act as intermediary in suing for peace terms. It left many Japanese in no doubt that they could not win the war, but there was still no guarantee that it would bring about capitulation. The Japanese rulers stuck to the view that as Emperor Hirohito had ordered the war in the first place, its prosecution was a divine imperative, which only Hirohito himself could rescind.

The deliberations at the Yalta conference in February 1945 produced historic effects, many of them unexpected. Soviet Russia had endured indescribable sufferings and losses during the war in Europe including 20 million killed. Stalin was determined to exact maximum reparation from his foes, which might now include Japan.

In Europe, reparations entailed removing everything of value that could be seized including the dismantling of factories to Russia for reassembly. Japan, however, had not been invaded so far and, in any case, there was doubt that there would be much left of Japanese industry or treasury in the wake of the B-29 incendiary raids.

Soviet policy, grounded firmly in *realpolitik*, instead demanded large territorial gains in Asia. This was Stalin's price for agreeing to join the war against Japan. The Allies came to view these aspects of the treaty with increasing suspicion and regret. Stalin had signed a non-aggression pact with the Germans in 1939 to avoid conflict but also agreed the division of Europe into vassal states between the Soviet Union and Nazi Germany. That was all about territorial gain, spheres of influence and buffer zones and was an insight into Soviet post-war priorities. Two years later in 1941 when the pact had broken down, Stalin signed a neutrality pact with Japan to secure his eastern regions while fighting Germany.

The Japanese treaty was still in force and, as mentioned, was honoured by Stalin until its expiry date in August 1945. The question at the time was whether he would make good his pledge to enter the Pacific war on its expiry, or before, or not at all. If Russia entered and attacked the Japanese armies and economic supply lines in Manchuria and China, this would be immensely valuable to the Allies, but only in the event of a decision by them actually to invade Japan. This decision had not yet been taken and, indeed, was growing more problematic. The Soviets had demonstrated that where their armies fought and won territory, they did not give it up. In this sense, time favoured the Soviets – the more time available to them, the more territory they were likely to gain whether it had been agreed at the Yalta Conference or not.

The toughest decision remained – that of the invasion of Japan with all the envisioned traumas. It was always a horrendous option, but a massive joint operation with the Allies invading from the south via Okinawa and Kyushu and the Soviets from the north via Manchuria, and the Sakhalin and Kuril Islands. Further concerns grew apace that stretched beyond winning the Pacific war to include how each of the strategic options would shape the post-war world. The priority was to end the war, but time was increasingly seen as crucial too. How would it be if the outcome of the war, distinguished by the bloodiest and most costly invasions in history, was critically diminished in the eyes of US citizens by agreement to a vast Soviet expansion into Asia?

The uneasy Allies were becoming distinct rivals. Winston Churchill too believed that the Soviets, having formalized their position on the winning side, were focused on the post-war world in Asia and how they could become a dominating power in the east. Churchill argued that there should now be no concessions made to Stalin for his support if that could be avoided, but it was not clear why Stalin would have agreed to such a shift, it having been agreed, and he might hold his armies back indefinitely. Having seen how developments had pitched the Allies into a dilemma whereby invasion options (with or without the Soviets) would be deeply problematic, what would be the alternatives?

Only naval blockade or aerial bombardment, conventional or atomic, could avoid the need for monstrous ground battles. Soviet involvement would reduce Allied losses and costs, but they would still be unimaginably grievous, and the Soviets would take over great tracts of territory in Asia. In any case, it would take much time for the Soviet forces to fight to a position of readiness to participate. This brought with it an additional worry, learned during the island-hopping phase. Given a pause, the Japanese were very effective in taking full advantage of it to strengthen their own preparations to repel future attack.

The outcome of all this deliberation (it could hardly be called decision) was that every option would be maintained against all possibilities until firmer and more focused decisions could be made. So it was agreed that, in the interim period, the Allies would continue to prepare and plan for an invasion, while other alternatives that would finish it without the need for invasion would be fervently pursued at the same time. What originally had been the central objectives of the Pacific War grand strategy was becoming a strategic backstop, to be used only if unavoidable.

There were a surprising number of alternatives. Firstly, the proponents of airpower argued that the B-29 could bring about the end of the war by incendiary bombing alone. The airpower option using the Boeing B-29 Superfortress to full extent needed no further deliberation. This aircraft was the ultimate delivery system of strategic destruction of the entire war. USAAF 21st Bomber Command, based in the Marianas, was now under the command of the pugnacious General Curtis LeMay, who characteristically made his presence felt from the start. He remained a fully paid-up disciple of the strategic theorist General Giulio Douhet, believing unswervingly that strategic bombing was both a necessary but also a sufficient condition to secure victory. All other armed forces were deemed auxiliary to that one effort, and in the B-29, he was confident that he had the aircraft that would, at last, make the point undeniably. General LeMay had been asked bluntly by his boss, General 'Hap' Arnold, when the war could be finished using strategic bombing. LeMay said that, provided he was allowed to go all out with incendiary raids, he could finish it before the end of September that year. Tokyo, as described, was razed to the ground in one raid which killed over 100,000 souls. At the height of the campaign, LeMay and his aircrew were reducing Japan at the rate of a city every day. It appeared that Douhet and his 20th Century adherents were to be proved right. Except that, even as LeMay was running out of targets to hit, the Japanese still showed no sign of surrendering. What if LeMay didn't get the result of which he was so confident? Where strategic bombing was concerned, errors of judgement had been made before, notably in Europe.

The USN took a longer view. It had been embattled since December 1941 but, after nearly four years of fighting, had prevailed and routed the IJN. With the enemy on the seas destroyed they could turn their efforts into completing a blockade, completely cutting off Japanese homeland supply lines. This finessing argued that the initiative should have been transferred back to the Allied navies with their surface vessels and submarines to continue sinking cargo shipping and tankers.

What of the submarines? Admiral Chester Nimitz, hero of Midway and one of the foremost naval strategists said,

> 'We shall never forget that it was our submarines that held the lines against the enemy while our fleets replaced losses and repaired wounds.'

Nimitz's gratitude bore testimony to the fact that they had always been there – undetected – screening the surface fleets from the enemy. When the IJN was no more a force to be reckoned with, the submarine service played a silent part in surrounding the Japanese islands with an undetectable patrol network. This eventually became impenetrable to commercial shipping. Japan had acquired by force an empire for the purpose of grabbing the raw materials that it lacked. Cut off from the spoils of exploitation from the lands it had conquered, it rapidly started to run out of everything, especially food, steel and oil. Like Great Britain, Japan comprises a group of islands situated off a continent. Anything that it needed and could not produce, or produce in sufficient quantity, had to be brought in by sea. The sea lanes were its jugular veins, and US submarines bit into them. This is exactly what German U-boats were attempting in both world wars, and in both nearly succeeded in strangling Great Britain. Winston Churchill's warning,

'If we lose the war at sea, we lose the war!'

applied as much to Japan as it did to Britain and for the same reasons.

The entire US submarine fleet was manned by numbers well below 2% of the total navy strength, but they sank over half of Japan's total wartime vessel losses. These included warships – battleships, heavy cruisers and no less than eight aircraft carriers. Submarines were small craft, easily, cheaply and quickly manufactured relative to other warships, capital ships in particular. That they punched way above their weight is extreme understatement. Notwithstanding their diminutive size, in numbers they were a paramount weapon system, capable of tearing away at surface shipping, no matter how mighty.

American Balao-class boats weighed around 1,500 tons, and the S-class boats only around 850 tons. The cost of each boat was around $3million and the United States' shipyards produced over 1,100 during the war. Surface capital ships, notably the obsolescent battleship and the new capital ships – aircraft carriers – cost orders of magnitude more money to produce. They took much longer to build and far more sailors to man and operate. Capital ships needed to be screened from air and underwater attack. To maintain their battle viability required them to be accompanied by flotillas of light cruisers, destroyers and light aircraft carriers with emplaned fighter aircraft and, of course, submarines.

Life aboard a 'sub' was not for the faint hearted. It was cramped and stinking of diesel and body odour. The diesel was the less repugnant. Submariners slowly gained a pallid colour through lack of sunlight.

Voices grew hoarse through throats breathing all kinds of strange gases and airborne bacteria. Beards grew because shaving seemed like an effete luxury. Periods of duty were exhausting because of the levels of concentration demanded, and because the consequences of making a mistake could mean the end. Coping postures emerged embracing, for example, an assumed piratical jauntiness. Like Royal Navy submarines, they often had a Jolly Roger hidden in the flag locker below for hoisting as they returned to harbour to report sinkings.

Submarines were, both tactically and strategically, war-winning offensive vessels. They were cheap to build and man, fast to produce, replace and repair. In coordinated formations, what the *Kriegsmarine* had called 'wolf-packs', they were deadly. They had the supreme underwater projectile in their magazines – torpedoes. Originating a hundred years previously, these innovations gradually eroded naval convention that you put against an enemy's warship one of your own of roughly equivalent size.

The United States Navy was largely 'dry' – alcohol was not to be had. However, like the character 'Beer Barrel' in James Michener's novel 'The Bridges at Toko-Ri', these pirates of the Pacific also used clever methods to smuggle a supply aboard to take the edge off the mental tensions on these men, which were severe to say the least. Authority turned a Nelsonian eye. When their 'tin fish' struck home there would come a jubilant release of joy and it all seemed worthwhile and a source of pride. But if they were taken by surprise by an enemy destroyer bearing straight at them at over thirty knots, firing depth charges and determined in the last event to ram, the horror is unimaginable.

When steam turbines were invented, anything you could not out-gun you had to be able to out-run, and anything you could not out-run you had to be able to out-gun. However, with reciprocating engines, there came prospect that a tiny craft such as a submarine, using surprise and stealth, could take on and disable battleships and aircraft carriers. Submarines were creatures of the night and of the depths. The torpedo-armed submarine had sufficient range and speed on the surface to track a warship undetected until in the best position to attack. Battleships were heavily armoured, but insufficiently to shrug off the destructive power of a well-aimed salvo of torpedoes. Firing a single torpedo, better still a salvo, at a surface ship stood a good chance of striking the target.

These characteristics – explosive power with the ability to close towards a vessel undetected – were a devastating combination. The submarine was hard to detect even after firing, and repeated attacks on convoys proved possible. Throughout the war in the Pacific, of the Japanese merchant marine seamen killed or wounded, over 90% were victims of attacks by US submarines. The Japanese, blinkered by the false precept that naval battles and wars could be finalized only by the outcomes of violent clashes between surface giants, neglected consideration of the capabilities of the submarine. It was arguably the most profound strategic mistake in the Imperial Japanese Navy's preparation for war.

By December 1944, the Japanese archipelago was surrounded by over 1,000 American submarines. They sank 600 merchant ships and cut in half Japan's import levels. Japan was thereby critically enfeebled industrially. Its population had begun to starve. With a naval blockade cutting supply lines and incendiary bombing from the air it should have been possible, the argument ran, to force an unconditional surrender without more hand-to-hand carnage as would occur in an invasion. Surrender, therefore, as an assured outcome, was simply a matter of waiting, but with the Soviet armies on the move, it seemed to the decision-makers that there was not enough time left.

Finally, there were the new atomic options that were close to ready for use. The existence of the new 'super-bombs' offered another type of alternative. That option, however, was so far untried but about to be tested. If it worked, it could be used without delay. It would cost little or nothing more in terms of the lives of Allied personnel. It was available without further significant cost in treasury. It would provide a test of its effects in a real war situation. Both strategic bombing options – incendiary bombing and atomic weapons – would avoid the need to invade with its casualties, costs, time requirements and sorrows. As the alliance between the US and the Soviet Union was now firmly focussed on the post-war consequences, the west's decision makers felt an increasing need to address these alternative strategies as quickly as possible. All things considered, the B-29 Superfortress strategic bomber might still be the best way to put an end to the Second World War.

Chapter 11

Making Choices

The pressure was on to make a decision that would produce a surrender and to get the war over as quickly as possible. The resolutions of the Yalta conference had been made ambiguous enough to produce apparent agreement, but also enough to be interpreted cynically in terms of the realities of international politics. This opened a divide between the post war objectives of the US government and the Soviet Union. Stalin, who has been described as a dictator who thought like an emperor, wished for a communist dominated world under the hegemony of Soviet Russia. The US wanted a world where liberal democracies would flourish. In the light of what was happening in Europe, a defeat of Japan that entailed Soviet Russia annexing vast chunks of Asia was now seen as a losing strategy in the longer run. The optimum solution for the US would have to be one that would address both these issues.

The death of President Franklin Delano Roosevelt (FDR) in April 1945 was deeply untimely. The leader of the western allies was highly popular, set to be President for a third term, and many believed irreplaceable. The war was not yet won and the west had lost their democratic giant. There was fear that the outcome of years of fighting, despite all effort and sorrow, would end badly without him.

The office of Vice Chairman was seen as little more than a sinecure, but one of the few constitutional functions was to step into the office of President should the incumbent die. Until the next election therefore, the new President would be Harry S. Truman, a Senator from the state of Missouri placed on the running ticket because he could deliver his home state at the polls. FDR had little time for him. He was from a humble profession with no experience or education in diplomacy or strategy. Truman himself stated that there must be a million people in the country more able to do the job than he, but he had been given the job and he was going to do it. He was quick to observe the actions of Stalin and draw the right conclusions about his territorial ambitions for a communist Europe as eastern European states began to be Sovietised and fall within the Soviet sphere of influence, soon to be known as the Soviet Bloc. The terms of the Yalta conference were being flouted. This was critical learning for a man who grew into a determined practitioner of *realpolitik* on the international stage. He was quick to realise that strategies involving a significant wait for Japan to capitulate, such as naval blockade, would win the Pacific war but at the expense of creating too much opportunity for Stalin's global territorial ambitions. He sailed for Europe in his allotted heavy cruiser, the USS Augusta, to attend the Potsdam conference on 7 July. The Augusta was escorted into the safety of the River Scheldt by HMS Hambledon, a Hunt Class destroyer (L37) in which the author's father was a young gunnery rating. He toured Berlin on the way, where he was appalled by the destruction. These would be fertile grounds for communist take-over, and he resolved to make good the damage in as much of Europe as could be done. He gave the responsibility to his Secretary of State – General George Marshall – and the Marshall Plan came about.

On 16 July the first nuclear device was tested at Los Alamos. The results were sent to Truman as soon as they had been analysed, and they arrived shortly after the conference had started. Truman now knew that the weapon would become a reality within days, and this was the news he was waiting for. It must have strengthened his resolve greatly. The conference went on and his aides witnessed the new President standing his ground on issues. Stalin, who had assumed he was up against a lightweight, noticed it too. Truman decided to let the other two leaders in on the secret – that this new super-weapon would be ready very soon. The British were already aware, but to Stalin the news was extremely unwelcome as he knew that this put him at a serous disadvantage vis a vis the US until the USSR also acquired such weapons.

The Potsdam Declaration on 2 August demanded immediate and unconditional surrender by the Japanese on pain of complete destruction. The Japanese government did not respond. The emperor, whose war it was, called for national solidarity and stated that the nation would remain under his control and that of his government. The government, however, remained riven between those who knew the war was lost and wished to limit further deaths and suffering and the military faction, who were demanding a fight to the death. The peace makers knew that opposing such fanaticism could be personally dangerous including the risk of assassination, and this stifled opposition. Truman returned to his cruiser and began the long journey back across the North Atlantic. Shortly after he sailed, he made his decision.

On 6 August a specially modified B-29 Superfortress dropped the first atomic bomb on Hiroshima. The city was razed to the ground and 150,000 people perished including those who died later from burns or radiation effects. The extent of the damage was reported to Hirohito but still evoked no surrender order. On 8 August, Russia declared war on Japan and commenced an invasion of Manchuria.

On 9 August another specially modified B-29 dropped a second bomb on Nagasaki, inflicting around 80,000 casualties. To the incredulity of the Allies there was still no reaction from the Japanese government. They were not aware of the cowed state of those in Japan wishing for peace. Hirohito was, however, in earnest consultation with his own advisors, as a result of which he decided to accept the Potsdam demands. The Japanese people heard the voice of their emperor for the first time when he announced on the radio that the war was over, and hostilities must cease. On 15 August the Japanese surrendered unconditionally.

Immediately after the surrender signing ceremony on 2 September 1945, presided over by General Douglas MacArthur on board the USS battleship Missouri, a flypast containing 462 B-29 Superfortresses flew over Tokyo Bay. The Pacific war was over.

Chapter 12

Epilogue

Stalin interpreted the use of the atomic bombs as a warning to the USSR that the US was now the predominant actor on the world stage. After withdrawing for a day to discuss this with his advisors, he decided to test Truman's metal. A message was sent to Truman indicating that he had reconsidered the former Russian territories that the Yalta agreement had ceded to him as an inducement to join the Allies in the Japanese war and had concluded that they were not enough. He requested that the US now agree to the 'reasonable request' for occupation of part of the northern Japanese island of Hokkaido by Soviet troops. He then added that refusal would not be acceptable. Truman recognized this as an aggressive try-on and responded peremptorily that the answer was no, and that was flat. It was the beginning of something much bigger.

Confounding the communisation of Europe, which was now progressing apace, became the priority. As the Allied countries celebrated the end of the war and the business of peacetime government was being reinstated, a diplomatic telegram arrived at the US State Department. It was from an American diplomat who had spent much time in Moscow. His name was George Kennan. The message was of historic import for the rest of the 20th century and was so lengthy that it was referred to as 'The Long Telegram'. In his message Kennan offered general principles relating to the Soviets based on a great deal of personal observation and experience. He stated that expansionism was a central principle of international communism. This was especially acute in the case of Soviet Russia because of recent history. Bonapartism in the19th century, and Nazism so recently in the 20th had produced a neurotic concern about being invaded, which aggravated their ideological determination to expand. The answer was for the west to stand firm and oppose defensively at all points. The Soviets, he declared, are impervious to the logic of reason, but very sensitive to the logic of force. If the west stands firm, the USSR will back down.

It is easy to see why this should have appealed to the new President. He had made one of the most important decisions of the era based on instinct. But now, from the realm of international diplomacy, here was an already developed evidence-based doctrine which made sense of it and gave it context. It was legitimised within a broad frame of reference, one which could be used to inform and guide future strategic policy. That policy became known as 'Containment'. George Kennan joined the group of President Truman's advisors. This administration established what came to be called the Truman Doctrine. This pledged American support for democratic nations against authoritarian threats, but in the first instance this meant communist expansion and gave rise to the Cold War. The North Atlantic Treaty Organization (NATO) was essentially a military alliance set up to deliver this policy in Europe. Under Article Five of the treaty, an attack on any member will trigger the immediate support, military, economic and diplomatic, of any treaty member attacked from outside. The Marshall Plan gave the economic means to rebuild Europe's economic base.

The formation of the United Nations provided a world-wide diplomatic theatre to prevent war and promote prosperity. However, it too had teeth. It authorized the military response to the communist incursions into South Korea in 1950 and could do so because the USSR was boycotting meetings of the presiding Security Council when it voted for intervention. It was not wise to be absent when such matters were being settled.

These precepts remained the central tenets of US foreign policy and strategic thinking for almost the rest of the 20th century. Its first manifestation was the flurry of Soviet espionage focused on stealing the US nuclear secrets that had produced the first two bombs. Truman was advised that it would take the Soviets ten years to develop such weapons, but due to espionage this was achieved in half that time. The first big test came in 1948 when Stalin cut off all supplies to Berlin, now an enclave inside the newly established communist East Germany. The western powers, principally the US and the UK, supplied the city by air for almost a year. The Soviets did not shoot down any of the aircraft being unwilling to risk escalation, and eventually backed down.

The next test came on the Korean Peninsula. Divided along the 38th parallel into North and South Koreas, the leader of North Korea, Kim Il-Sung, wished to reunite the country under communist rule. Previously refusing permission, Stalin eventually gave it in 1950. North Korean troops drove into the south pushing back the Republic of Korea (ROK) army until, with the small US contingent stationed there, they were penned up in a small area around the coastal city of Pusan. This was opposed by B-29s flying out of Okinawa, which bombed infrastructure such as bridges and road crossings. The newly formed United Nations poured in reinforcements, which, combined with a remarkable flanking invasion from the sea at Inchon under the command of General MacArthur of Philippines fame, rolled the entire communist army back to the Yalu River. Air power was key in this conflict with thousands of tactical strikes delivered by allied aircraft carriers steaming up and down on station off the coasts. The strategic bombing was principally undertaken by squadrons of B-29

Superfortresses. The Yalu river was the boarder with communist China, who then intervened in turn to push the front line south again.

The war was fought to a standstill after three years and both Koreas settled down to glare at each other from either side of the 38th parallel, where it all began. No peace treaty has ever been signed formally ending the war.

Containment as a policy doctrine continued up until 1990, when Premier Gorbachev, concluding there may be a better way than competing with the United States in a ruinously expensive arms race, introduced the concepts of Glasnost and Perestroika, which ended the Cold War bringing a new relief to international tensions. This fragile entente cordial did not last long into the 21st century. The world today feels closer to the Cold War again, but this time with the complication of multiple nuclear-armed players.

Containment wars continued, with proxy wars being fought by the vassal states of both powers. The biggest and most notorious was the Vietnam conflict. Before this the jet age had rendered the B-29 obsolete. Losses in Korea to MiG 15 jet fighters found the B-29 forced back to attacking at night. The most advanced, expensive, and arguably the best piston-engine propellor strategic bomber ever built, faded into history. Its relegation, ironically, was delayed by the Soviets reverse-engineering four machines damaged in the Pacific war, which had diverted to Russian airfields. This project was completed in two years and emerged in the form of the Tupolev Tu-4. It gave the USSR the nuclear delivery system necessary for it to declare itself a nuclear power. Code-named 'Bull', it was almost an exact replica of the B-29 externally, although unlikely to have incorporated some of the more advanced technical features. It gave the 'B-29' a bizarre further lease of life batting for the other side.

Development of the gas turbine marked the end of the era of piston aeroengines in large aircraft such as heavy bombers and airliners.

The airscrew or propellor lasted a few years longer, the Convair B-36 having six of them, but they too were relegated to smaller aircraft by the arrival of turbojet and turbofan engines. The B-29 was modified, firstly into a heavy freighter dubbed C-97 Stratofreighter. This marque was further modified into an airliner designated the 377 Stratocruiser. It was a brave venture. It had long range, high altitude performance, unmatched luxury, two decks, and its cabins were pressurised. Alas, it was not a success. It was eye-wateringly expensive to operate and maintain, affordable by few, but mostly because it was plagued by a series of fatal accidents due to propellor and engine failures. It could not match competition in the form of the newer Lockheed Constellation family. By the end of the 1950s it was all over with the arrival of turbojet airliners such as the Boeing 707 and the Douglas DC-8.

The B-29 had an incredibly intense career. It was brief, but it stood like no other aircraft in the history of aviation.